Two new Worlds

Crown 8vo. Price 5s. net

With Portrait of Dr. Stoney, and 35 Diagrams in the Text.

THE ELECTRON THEORY

A POPULAR INTRODUCTION TO THE NEW THEORY OF ELECTRICITY AND MAGNETISM

By E. E. FOURNIER d'ALBE, B.Sc. (Lond.), A.R.C.Sc.

WITH A PREFACE BY

G. JOHNSTONE STONEY, M.A., D.Sc., F.R.S.

"It is called a work of popularisation. But let there be no mistake: the author has here done truly scientific work."—*Journal de Physique*.

"The best possible introduction to modern views of electricity."—*Medical Electrology*.

"An easily-read rendering of an abstruse subject."—*Electrical Magazine*.

"A lucid popular account of the main outlines of the electron theory as it exists at the present day."—*Spectator*.

"Mr. Fournier meets a distinct want in supplying a little volume which explains the electron theory of magnetism and electricity in a simple yet scientific manner."—*Pall Mall Gazette*.

"Mr. Fournier d'Albe has been more than successful in presenting his simple and lucid account of the new theory of electricity and magnetism; and it is not too much to say that it is just the book that was wanted, and we heartily recommend it to the notice of our readers."—*Electricity*.

"A remarkable book, and one which contains a world of suggestion for all who are concerned with electrical affairs, is Mr. E. E. Fournier's new treatise on the 'Electron Theory,' a popular introduction to the new theory of electricity and magnetism."—*Page's Weekly*.

"Mr. Fournier has done electricians a great service in writing this book. Its title is too small, as it is really a book on 'electricity and magnetism' treated from the electron point of view. This is just what has been wanted for some little time."—*Electrician*.

"Mr. Fournier d'Albe, who has been long and favourably known as a compiler of a weekly *chronique* on electrical matters, may be congratulated upon being the first in the field with a complete statement in English of the electronic theory."—*The Athenæum*.

"This work gives an easily understood and very able treatment of the whole subject of the electron theory, which deserves to be sincerely recommended as introductory literature."—*Physikalische Zeitschrift*.

"A glance at the table of contents of this book is sufficient to show that it fills an acute want at the present time. It attempts the consistent application of the all-embracing electron theory in an elementary manner to the whole range of electro-magnetic phenomena. In making this attempt the author is to be congratulated both on the choice of his subject and the skill and originality he has displayed in accomplishing it. . . . Few possess the necessary qualifications for a task which covers such a wide range of subjects, and, so far as we know, this is the first time it has been seriously attempted. The book is therefore unique, and should prove of value to the student, the teacher, and the investigator."—*Nature*.

LONGMANS, GREEN, AND CO.

LONDON, NEW YORK, BOMBAY, AND CALCUTTA

TWO NEW WORLDS

BY THE SAME AUTHOR

THE ELECTRON THEORY

A POPULAR INTRODUCTION TO THE
NEW THEORY OF ELECTRICITY
AND MAGNETISM

With a Preface by
G. JOHNSTONE STONEY, M.A., D.Sc., F.R.S.

With Frontispiece Portrait of Dr. Stoney,
and 35 Diagrams in the Text

Crown 8vo, 5s. net

LONGMANS, GREEN, AND CO.
LONDON, NEW YORK, BOMBAY, AND CALCUTTA

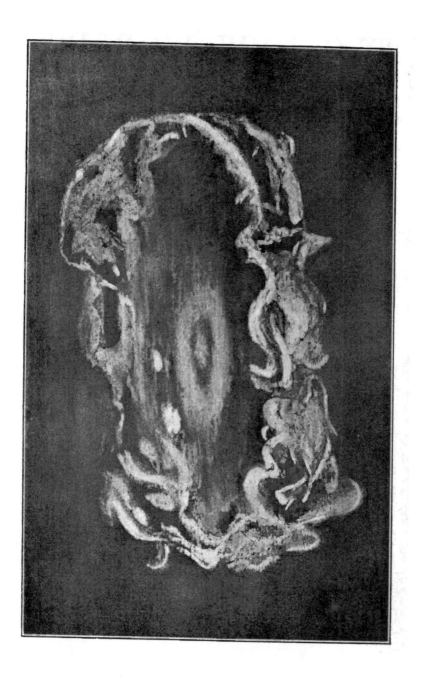

TWO NEW WORLDS

I. THE INFRA-WORLD
II. THE SUPRA-WORLD

BY

E. E. FOURNIER D'ALBE, B.Sc.
AUTHOR OF "THE ELECTRON THEORY"

LONGMANS, GREEN, AND CO.
39 PATERNOSTER ROW, LONDON
NEW YORK, BOMBAY, AND CALCUTTA
1907

PREFACE

THE following pages contain an attempt to penetrate the mystery of space and time with the help of the most modern resources of scientific research. The treatment extends to the Infinite on one side and the Infinitesimal on the other, and seeks to annex a "first order" of each to the vast realm already surveyed and partly controlled by the human intellect. The main thesis of this work is that a universe constructed on a pattern not widely different from ours is encountered on a definite and measurable scale of smallness, and another on a correspondingly larger scale. To these universes I give the names Infra-World and Supra-World respectively.

In studying the characteristics of these two new worlds—"new" in the sense of being now for the first time discovered and described—I have taken for my basis that last and greatest generalisation of science known as the "electron theory," which has during the last ten years of triumphant progress accounted for all known phenomena of electricity and magnetism, and thus placed the whole of physical science on a new and firm foundation. The new point of view introduced into this theory for the purposes of the present research is confined to the stipulation that matter and electricity are quantities of an essentially different nature, and that whatever they may be, one of them cannot be interpreted in terms of the other. There is, in fact, no "electric theory of matter," and a further simplification of natural laws must proceed on non-material lines.

For the philosophical doctrines guiding these researches I am very greatly indebted to my revered master and friend, Dr. Johnstone Stoney, F.R.S., whose ontological speculations have profoundly influenced and enlightened me. Ontology is a subject left uncultivated by most modern men of science, and that may account for the somewhat materialistic tendency of most of their writings when touching on philosophical subjects. The science of the mind is as yet in its infancy, largely on account of the lack of a comprehensive theory of mental phenomena. Mental pathology and psychical research will enter on a career of useful achievement as soon as they can agree upon a "point of view." At present all is chaos and guesswork. The Kepler and Newton of the soul are still awaited.

A work like the present necessarily appeals to the intellect in the first instance. But the proof of the existence of two worlds whose possibility was barely suspected hitherto, and whose connection with ourselves, with our own past and future, may be very intimate, must also stir the heart and fire the imagination. I have carefully avoided entering the field of theological controversy, but I hope that those who believe that this world of ours is in good hands, that it is not governed by blind chance or inflexible destiny, that it offers infinite possibilities of faith and hope and love, will derive some additional comfort and encouragement from the following pages, even though these proceed from a dry analysis of known facts. May this, together with the circumstances of this book being written in Ireland and largely inspired by Irish thoughts and thinkers, go to justify its Irish motto: "For the Glory of God and the Honour of Ireland."

E. E. FOURNIER D'ALBE.

CHAPELIZOD, *June* 1907.

b

CONTENTS

I. THE INFRA-WORLD

II. THE SUPRA-WORLD

Do cum glóine Dé
agus onóra na h-Éireann

I

THE INFRA-WORLD

TWO NEW WORLDS

CHAPTER I

A NEW MICROCOSM

1. To throw the image of a drop of stagnant water on a screen under a high magnifying power, and to reveal the intense and manifold life which pervades that aqueous microcosm, is a favourite proceeding of the popular science lecturer. It never fails to fascinate the audience, and often terrifies it. There is something uncanny in the thought that a dew-drop may contain thousands of small animals which eat, and fight, and love, and die, and whose span of life, to judge from their intense activity, is probably filled with as many events as our own. But some consolation may be derived from the reflection that, when the water is boiled, all that life disappears, and nothing remains but dead matter—organic, maybe, but no longer organised or furnished with a complete set of emotions, sensations, and purposes.

But what guarantee have we that an instrument of much higher power than the microscope—an instrument as far superior to the microscope as the microscope is superior to the naked eye—may not reveal further worlds of hitherto unsuspected life, which may possibly be more difficult to destroy than the minute organisms of the pond?

The smallest object which can be distinctly perceived by the normal human eye at a distance of 10 in. is $\frac{1}{250}$ in. in diameter; or, more strictly speaking, when two black objects are separated by a bright interval $\frac{1}{250}$ in. wide, they are perceived as separate objects.

Now a good microscope magnifies about two hundred times, so that the limit of resolving power is brought down to $\frac{1}{50000}$ in. This is sufficient for practically all purposes for which the microscope is usually intended. A human blood corpuscle is $\frac{1}{3200}$ in. in diameter, and is therefore a very large object for a powerful microscope. Of yeast-cells there are 3000 to the inch, and the amœba is of the same size. The spores of some fungi are as many as 6000 or even 8000 to the inch, whereas the spores of the anthrax bacillus are not more than $\frac{1}{24000}$ in. in diameter. The markings of diatoms are considered somewhat exacting test-objects for good microscopes, and 30,000 of them have been counted to the inch, and the same size must be assigned to the bacilli of tuberculosis.

Small as these objects are, they do not represent the extreme limits of microscopic vision.

Abbé has calculated that the utmost attainable limit of resolving power can never exceed $\frac{1}{113000}$ in., on account of diffraction. This means that when objects are any smaller than that, and are viewed by light transmitted along the axis of the micro- scope, the light bends round the object, and enters the eye just as if the object did not exist. Hence the object is invisible. This difficulty could be overcome if photographs could be obtained by extreme ultra-violet light, which, on account of the shortness of its constituent waves, is less bent aside from its rectilinear course.

But diffraction is not an unmixed curse of optics. It may be utilised for ultra-microscopic vision. Of this there are two familiar examples. The fixed stars show no measurable diameter, even with the highest magnifying power. They would be quite invisible but for the fact that a parallel beam of light, incident upon the eye or upon any other achromatic instrument, is not brought to a focus in a geometrical point, but in a small disc produced by diffraction, a disc sufficiently large to come within the perceptive power of the retina.

The motes floating in a sunbeam, again, would be quite invisible but for diffraction. They are less than $\frac{1}{100000}$ in. in diameter, as can be proved by their rate of settling down in still air. Their very smallness enables them to scatter the light in a lateral direction. A microscope has been constructed on this principle of lateral illumination by Siedentopf and Szigmondy,[1] and by its means objects only a millionth of an inch in diameter have been perceived. We cannot say that these objects have been "seen." But their presence has been indicated by what might be called diffractive symbols, appearances serving to indicate their presence in the field of vision, just as distant smoke indicates a fire. Thus, when in the "ultra-microscope" we perceive an object surrounded by rings, we know that we have to do with a very minute body. We can count such bodies, and observe their motions and changes of size and arrangement. The inventors of the ultra-microscope used their instrument for determining the weight of the particles of gold contained in a colloid solution of that substance.

The world revealed by the ultra-microscope is not a living world. No organisms can fall short of a certain size and live. Life appears to require a certain minimum of molecules to support it. The physical processes of life are so manifold that a single molecule, or even a million molecules, are unable to compass them.

No man has yet seen a molecule; but countless experiments and indirect measurements have given us a fair idea of their size and weight, and we

[1] *Annalen der Physik*, No. 1, 1903.

can determine with a very considerable degree of accuracy the number of molecules which go to make up a living organism.

One of the smallest infusoria known is the Monas Dallingeri, which is only $\frac{1}{6000}$ in. in diameter. At a certain stage of the life-history of this organism, two individuals combine and fuse into one, and after six hours' incubation give rise to a large number of spores whose size is not accurately known, but which cannot be more than $\frac{1}{60000}$ in. Each of these spores is an independent living individual.

It is not at all difficult to arrive at an estimate of the number of molecules which go to make up that spore, but before doing so, it will be worth while to translate our dimensions into the metric system. The unit adopted in measuring objects of the size of a wave-length of light is the micro-millimetre, or millionth of a millimetre, denoted by the symbol $\mu\mu$. In ordinary microscopic work the micron, μ, or thousandth of a millimetre, is now more generally adopted. It is useful to remember that 25·4 millimetres, or 25,400,000 micromillimetres, or 25,400 microns, go to the inch, so that one of the spores under discussion is about half a micron in diameter, or 423 $\mu\mu$. Now the average diameter of the molecules constituting the substance of the spore has been estimated at 0·3 $\mu\mu$, so that we see that a chain

of some 1200 such molecules would reach from
one end of it to the other. But we also know
that the molecules do not all touch each other.
The specific gravity of the spore is nearly equal to
that of water, and in water the molecules are
sufficiently widely apart to allow of their free
motion about each other. No doubt the various
parts of the cytoplasm, nucleus, and cell-wall of
the spore consist of various intricate groupings
and aggregations of molecules; but, on the average,
we may estimate that the molecules are half a $\mu\mu$
apart, so that a cubic space of $\frac{1}{8}$ cubic $\mu\mu$ goes to
each molecule. Since the radius is about 200 $\mu\mu$
the volume of the spore is $\frac{4}{3}r^3\pi$, or 33,500,000
cubic $\mu\mu$. Multiplying this by eight, we get 268
million as the number of molecules constituting the
spore.

This number, roughly approximate as it is,
enables us to draw the important conclusion that
*no living organism contains less than a hundred
million molecules.*

When, therefore, we penetrate further into the
realms of ultra-microscopy, we leave life behind,
and have to do with none but unorganised matter.
We can perceive the presence of objects down to
about 20 $\mu\mu$ in diameter, which cannot contain
more than about 50,000 molecules. Beyond that
limit, even the most recent optical devices fail us,
and we must fall back upon the visualising powers

of the scientific imagination, trusting that optical progress will some day enable us to verify our imaginings by ocular demonstration.

2. As our resolving powers increase, the world of small things becomes more and more unfamiliar. If the ordinary microscope reveals beings whose existence on a large scale would be impossible, how shall we find our way in a world whose objects are of molecular dimensions? But since we have started on that venturesome journey, let us go straight ahead, and endeavour to find some link between the new kingdom of Lilliput and our own universe.

When we arrive within sight of the molecule, the microcosm becomes invisible by ordinary means, as already stated. But, as we shall see, there is no reason why it should be invisible to eyes properly adapted to its scale of magnitude.

Fortunately for us, that scale of magnitude is known with sufficient accuracy to prevent our making any very grave blunders in finding our way in the infra-world. We know that the atoms are about 0·6 $\mu\mu$ in diameter, and that they are surrounded by electrons in some such way as our sun is surrounded by planets. These electrons have a diameter of a millionth of a micro-millimetre, or 10^{-13} cm. Now, the diameter of the earth is 12×10^{8} cm. Hence the ratio of the size of the earth to the size of the electron is $1·2 \times 10^{22}$, or approximately 10,000 trillions to 1. This ratio appears to be of fundamental importance. It is nothing less than the *ratio of the scales of successive universes.*

Since in the minute world we are now exploring atoms correspond to suns, and electrons to planets, we may boldly equate our earth to an electron, and find how far the analogy holds good.

Time and space are, after all, purely relative. If, at midnight to-night, all things, including ourselves and our measuring instruments, were reduced in size 1000 times, we should be left quite unaware of any such change. There would be nothing to prove that it had taken place. Also, if all events and all timepieces were accelerated in the same ratio, we should be equally ignorant of the event. We measure size by our own bodies or by the size of the earth. We measure time by the rotation of the earth or by its revolution round the sun.

Now, if we were small enough to live on an electron as we now do on the earth, we should measure all things by comparing them with ourselves or with our electron, and we should measure time by the rotation of our electron or its revolution round the central atom. Now, the period of the earth's revolution about the sun is 3×10^7 seconds (= one year), whereas the period of revolution of the average electron round its atom is 2×10^{-15} seconds. The ratio of these two periods is $1 \cdot 5 \times 10^{22}$, or substantially the same as the ratio of the diameters. Hence in the infra-world *space and time are reduced in the same proportion.*

It is this curious circumstance which justifies the expression "infra-world." It shows that the world in which an electron is equivalent to the earth is a real microcosm, a "visible universe" on an almost inconceivably small scale, but still a universe where conditions do greatly resemble our own.

Our visible universe consists of stars strewn irregularly through space. As we descend in the scale of dimensions, we first enter the region of micro-organisms, then the region of molecular aggregates, and, lastly, the region of atoms and electrons, and it is only at the last stage that we find any conditions comparable with those of our world.

When, with our own progressive diminution, the small things appear larger and larger, when finally the electron comes to resemble the earth, and we take our stand on it as "infra-men" 10^{22} times smaller than our present size, we enter this mysterious infra-world, and begin to appreciate its real structure. Our electron turns out to be a hard sphere, but sufficiently varied in its surface (most likely) to present what we used to call landscape effects. This means but a slight irregularity of the surface, so slight as to be impossible to trace by terrestrial measurements.

We may have entered the infra-world in the full

expectation of finding everything in a wild whirl and turmoil, and here we find ourselves entirely mistaken. Our electron rolls through space as leisurely and majestically as the earth appeared to do. When one revolution is completed, another is begun; and so it goes on for a thousand million "years" perhaps—years measured by the revolutions of the electron. This vast period covers but a millionth of one terrestrial second, it is true, but how could we know that? We no longer measure time by the terrestrial scale. We measure it on the same principle, but our scale is reduced 10^{22} times; and if we could measure the earthly year, it would appear to us to be an immense period stretching over 10,000 trillion infra-years.

We could still talk about a speed of 1 cm. per second, but since the centimetre would be derived from the electron instead of the earth, it would be 10^{-22} of a terrestrial centimetre. It should, therefore, be called an "infra-centimetre." The new second should also be called an "infra-second." But velocities so measured would be really equal if measured in the same figures. Thus, a velocity of 1 infra-cm. per infra-second is exactly equal to a velocity of 1 cm. per second. And another of the curious coincidences brought out by this speculation is that the velocities prevalent in both worlds *are substantially the same, both relatively and absolutely.*

We talk of "planetary" and "cosmic" velocities, and find that most stars have a speed of $3\frac{1}{2}$ million cm. per second. Now, this is just about equal to the speed of the average electron in its orbit. We need not, therefore, do any violence to our notions of possible speeds in descending into the infra-world. It is generally thought that no matter can move with a speed exceeding the velocity of light—viz., 3×10^{10} cm. per second. It is therefore reassuring to find that the speeds of the infra-world are well below that limit.

3. *Infra-Light.*—It is evident that whatever may be the constitution of any infra-organisms which may people our infra-world, that world cannot be to them what ours is to us without the existence of light. That light cannot, of course, be what we understand by the term. It cannot be earthly light, for a single vibration of earthly light takes a whole "year" to accomplish itself in the infra-world. But the infra-world, if it is like ours, must consist of particles—atoms and electrons, maybe—of a still smaller order of magnitude, another 10^{22} times smaller than the infra-planets; and the motion of these infra-electrons lights up the infra-world. Since all speeds remain the same, the speed of propagation of infra-light will be 3×10^{10} cm. per second, like our terrestrial light. But any Rœmer or Foucault or Fizeau among the infra-men would actually obtain the same figure for the velocity of

infra-light by the observation of some infra-Jupiter's satellites, or the twirling of some infra-mirror. The luminiferous ether, therefore, may be taken to remain the same in both worlds. Mysterious as ever, it is the one substance which is always with us, and ever the same.

CHAPTER II

THE FORCES OF THE INFRA-WORLD

1. WE have seen that in the infra-world, the world where atoms and electrons stand for suns and planets, the absolute velocities are of the same order as those in our world, but that all lengths and times are reduced in the same proportion—viz. 10^{22} to 1.

From these data we can, without further trouble, deduce that all surfaces are reduced in the ratio of 10^{44} to 1, and all volumes in the ratio 10^{66} to 1.

But there are a large number of other quantities, apart from these geometrical and kinematical quantities, and it will be of interest to consider in what proportion they are reduced or increased in descending to the infra-world.

The most important of these is *mass*, or the quantity of inertia opposed by a body to a given moving force. If densities were of the same order in both worlds, masses would be reduced to the same extent as volumes—viz., in the ratio of 10^{66} to 1. This, however, is not the rule in the solar system, where Jupiter has only about one-fourth of the density of the earth, and the sun is specifically lighter even than that. Thus we may expect bodies

to be denser in the infra-world than in our world.
Now, the mass of the earth is approximately 10^{28}
grammes, whereas that of an electron is about 10^{-27}
grammes. The ratio is 10^{55}, so that in this case the
mass is only reduced by that ratio, while the volume
is reduced 10^{66} times. This means that the density
is increased nearly a billion times.

This is nothing to be surprised at, and becomes
inevitable when we consider that our densities
are determined by measurements and estimates
made in the case of solid "bodies," consisting, as
every one now admits, of discrete particles separated
by more or less wide intervals. These intervals
are usually imperceptibly small. Solid copper
consists of atoms and atomic aggregates tightly
packed as close as they will go at a given temperature. But this does not mean that the atoms
are always in contact. It only implies that when
the atoms are pressed together still more tightly
forces are brought into play — internal kinetic
forces most likely—which resist any further diminution of volume. An atom may, for all that, resemble a swarm of bees, which cannot be compressed
with impunity.

Still, the atom has a certain mass, and this must
be inherent in its constituents—that is to say, the
electrons or other particles of which it is composed.
If these are, as we have found, a billion times
more dense than ordinary matter, it follows that

only one part in a billion of the "volume" of an atom need be filled up by them.

In view of the fact that the volumes of the sun and all the planets put together fill up just about one-billionth of the solar system within the orbit of Neptune, the analogy between an atom and a solar system becomes more strikingly evident. But this part of the analogy is really implied in the hypothesis that all lengths are reduced in the same proportion.

2. The superior density of the "celestial bodies" of the infra-world implies that when they are set in motion they have a billion times more kinetic energy, volume for volume, than the planets of our system. If, therefore, we were suddenly transported into the infra-world, we should know by this, without any other indication, that circumstances had changed. But we should soon find out other and more fundamental differences. The cosmic velocities are, as we have seen, practically the same in both worlds, both absolutely and as measured by the standards of each world independently. This is due to the fact that a velocity is the ratio of a space to a time, or LT^{-1}. If both L and T are changed in the same ratio, the result remains the same, and it remains the same, too, when the unit is changed to the same extent in both L and T. But an acceleration is a length divided by the square of a time, and if the units of both space and time are

B

10^{22} times smaller, the same absolute acceleration, measured first in our world and then in the infra-world, will appear 10^{22} smaller in the second case than in the first.

To give an illustration:—A body acquires on earth a velocity of 981 cm. per second in one second under the action of the earth's gravitational force. The acceleration is, therefore, 981 units. Now measure the same acceleration in the infra-world. One centimetre becomes 10^{22} cm., one second becomes 10^{22} seconds, and a velocity of 10^{22} cm. per 10^{22} seconds is unit velocity, as on earth. But this unit velocity is acquired in one earthly second, which in the infra-world is drawn out to 10^{22} infra-seconds, or about 100 billion infra-years, and our normal acceleration will therefore appear to be so slight as to be imperceptible. It will be something comparable with the acceleration of a building gradually subsiding into the earth, and being buried in the course of untold ages.

It follows that if the inhabitants of the infra-world define acceleration by our methods, *their* unit acceleration must be prodigious in our eyes, amounting, as it does, to 10^{22} of our units.

The time-keepers of the infra-world are the stars of the infra-heavens, or what we call the atoms. The infra-planets, *alias* electrons, revolve round the infra-suns, *alias* atoms, as much more frequently as they are smaller than our planets and suns respectively. This is a purely kinematical theorem; but in order to account for it dynamically, we must consider the forces at work in the infra-world.

Now, centrifugal force is proportional to the square of the velocity of the revolving body, and inversely proportional to its distance from the centre of attraction. In symbols, $F = \frac{mV^2}{R}$ where m is the mass, V the velocity, and R the radius of the orbit. Now, in descending into the infra-world, V remains substantially the same, m is reduced 10^{55} times, and R is reduced 10^{22} times. Hence the centrifugal force is reduced to 10^{-33} times the force, say, between the earth and the sun.

How is this force balanced? The distance between two bodies in the infra-world is 10^{22} times less than between two bodies in this world, and hence the gravitational force must be multiplied by 10^{44}. But, on the other hand, the gravitational force is proportional to the product of the masses, which are both reduced 10^{55} times. Hence the gravitational attraction is in the infra-world $\frac{10^{-55} \times 10^{-55}}{10^{-44}}$, or only 10^{-66} times what it is with us. This is 10^{33} times too small to balance even the reduced centrifugal force of 10^{-33} dynes found above. Still, if our dynamical principles hold good—and everything we know points in that direction—we may be sure that that attractive force of 10^{-33} dynes is somehow provided. But this requires that all *central* forces in the infra-world are increased 10^{33} times, in order to account dynamically for the motions we actually observe.

We may therefore tabulate the various units in the two worlds as follows:—

In the infra-world the unit of

Length is reduced	10^{22} times.
Time is reduced	10^{22} ,,
Velocity is unchanged .	
Mass is reduced	10^{55} ,,
Area is reduced	10^{44} ,,
Volume is reduced	10^{66} ,,
Acceleration is increased . . .	10^{22} ,,
Mechanical force is reduced . .	10^{33} ,,
Density is increased	10^{11} ,,

The above calculations may appear somewhat abstruse, and the immense quantities denoted by the exponential figures may appal some readers who are not used to deal with figures on that scale. But it should be remembered not only that such figures enter into the daily calculations of astronomers, who practise what is acknowledged to be the most exact of all sciences, but that their manipulation, once acquired, is extremely easy and peculiarly elegant. We are dealing with quantities on a very small, instead of a very large, scale, and the exponential notation enables us to "think in millions" (or in millionths) with the same ease and certainty as we experience in dealing with the simple multiplication table. As a rule, indeed, our operations are confined to addition and subtraction.

3. We have now laid a solid foundation for our knowledge of this newly-discovered world. We see that, while the *appearances* remain the same, the *central forces* must necessarily be different, and must, indeed, vastly exceed the mechanical forces we are familiar with. If we take the visible universe as it is, and reduce all its dimensions in the same ratio, and accelerate the rates of revolution of the various celestial bodies in the same ratio, so as to keep their absolute velocities the same as before, we find that this cannot be done with the simple gravitational attraction as we know it. We must have a more powerful centripetal force.

We can give a simple illustration in the case of the earth and the moon. Let all their dimensions be halved, and let their velocities and densities remain the same as before. Then, since the volume of each body will be one-eighth of what it was, its mass also will be one-eighth, and the gravitational attraction, being proportional to the product of the masses, will be $\frac{1}{64}$th of the present attraction. On the other hand, their distance will also be halved, and this will increase the gravitational attraction four times. So that on the whole we have a centripetal force one-sixteenth of the present force.

As regards the centrifugal force, this is proportional to $\frac{mV^2}{R}$, and depends only upon the revolving body. Now V is the same as before, m is reduced eight times, and R is halved. Hence, on the whole, the centrifugal force will be one-fourth of the present force which keeps the moon in its orbit. But it will be four times too large for the very feeble gravitational attraction, and so the moon will fly off into space.

The fact that, though such a proportional reduction is made in the world of atoms and electrons, yet the electrons revolve about their atoms in orbits whose existence is demonstrated by every ray of light, shows that the central forces must greatly exceed the Newtonian attraction.

We know what this new central force is. *It is the force of electrostatic attraction.* We might almost say that it is specially designed to make possible the existence of an infra-world on the pattern of our own universe, but on a very minute scale. Incidentally, the electric force produces a variety of interesting terrestrial phenomena. But, essentially, it may fitly be described as the "gravitation of the infra-world."

CHAPTER III

LIFE IN THE INFRA-WORLD

1. WE have seen that if orbital motions resembling the earth's motion round the sun are to be preserved on a molecular scale—the scale of the infraworld—and if the absolute orbital velocities are to be of the same order in each case, centripetal forces must be at work which greatly exceed the gravitational force we are accustomed to. Such a centripetal force, enormous in comparison with gravitational force, we are already familiar with in the case of electrostatic attraction. When one electron is placed at a distance of 1 cm. from another, it repels it with a force of about 10^{-19} dynes. By virtue of their ponderable masses, the two electrons at the same time attract each other with a force of about 10^{-62} dynes. In this case, therefore, the electric force exceeds the gravitational force 10^{43} times. This enormous difference shows at once that as soon as electric forces come into play we are amply provided with machinery for producing the necessary speed of revolution. But it has been objected that such prodigious forces as these would break up any structure with which we are acquainted,

and that our imagination recoils helplessly from any attempt to picture an electron as it really is. That this attitude is quite mistaken I hope to show in what follows.

2. We have found that the electric forces "make the world go round" in the infra-world. But before we can prove the complete analogy between an atom with its electrons and our solar system, several objections remain to be dealt with. These are—

(1) An electron, having such a prodigious charge in comparison with its mass and size, could not be held together by any known force.

(2) If there are several electrons revolving about an atom, they would seriously perturb each other by their mutual repulsions.

As regards the first objection, it is best answered by a comparison with the earth. Who would suspect that the earth is negatively charged to a potential of a billion volts? Yet so it is, as can be easily proved from the data of atmospheric electricity. The earth's charge is certainly not less than 10^{18} electrostatic units. It surface density of electrification is just about one electrostatic unit per square centimetre, meaning that 2930 million free electrons are distributed over every square centimetre of its surface. And yet we find no electric phenomena in ordinary objects around us. The charges are there all the same. But they pass into the atmosphere and back into the earth, and all we know of them as a rule is confined to thunderstorms and auroras.

In the case of the electron, with its charge of $3\cdot4 \times 10^{-10}$ units and its radius of about 10^{-13} cm., the potential is only a million volts. But the surface density is much greater, being about 10^{16} units per square centimetre. Hence the electric field just above the surface is 10^{16} times the field above the surface of the earth. No cohesive force known to us could withstand that strain. But then it must be remembered that the density of an electron is 10^{11} times the density of the earth. Therefore cohesive force is 10^{22} times stronger than on earth, and this is amply able to protect the electron from disintegration by its own electric forces.

These considerations have the effect of making the electron more and more familiar. We have indeed here, for the first time, a rational view of an electron, based upon conceptions familiar in our own world, and introducing no new and unknown forces. The forces are much greater than ours, but then we have already for some time been acquainted with the greatness of molecular forces, and these molecular forces are the forces at play in what we call the infra-world. We only apply common sense and elementary science to these minute particles, whose existence is revealed to us by all the phenomena of physics and chemistry.

So far, then, we are on solid ground. The electron turns out to be something like our own earth, only that electric force takes the place of gravitational force in orbital motions. Our "molecular" forces, such as cohesion and rigidity, have their analogue in the cohesive forces of the "infra-molecules," those particles of an order 10^{22} times smaller than our molecules, which account for the molecular phenomena of the infra-world, and explain the resistance of the electron to electric disruption.

As regards objection (2), it should be borne in mind that there is no essential difference between perturbation by repulsion and perturbation by attraction, such as is the rule in our own solar system. That such perturbations actually take place is shown by the complicated character of the spectra of most elements. These spectra would consist of a few single lines, as in the hydrogen spectrum, if the electrons revolved round the atoms quite independently of each other. But the permanence of the lines shows also that the perturbations are compensated, as in the solar system, and do not produce a permanent disturbance of the orbits. It must also be remembered that at high velocities the mutual repulsion between two electrons is largely balanced by electro-dynamic attraction. When two similarly charged bodies move side by side through the ether, their electrostatic repulsion is balanced to some extent by their electro-magnetic attraction—the extent depends upon the speed. The electro-magnetic attraction is the same fraction of the electrostatic repulsion as the speed of the bodies is of the speed of light. Now the speed of electrons, although of the same *order* of magnitude as the speed of the earth, is, as a rule, about a hundred times greater, and has been known to attain a value one-third the velocity of light. This would reduce the repulsion of two electrons moving abreast to two-thirds of their repulsion when standing still.

3. An interesting question arises as to what constitutes the charge of an electron, and what conditions determine its size. We know that the facts of electricity are fully accounted for by the existence of electrons of constant mass and charge. The explanation of the esoteric nature of electric charges is thus pushed a stage further back. It is not really accomplished, any more than mass is explained by the atomic theory. This in no way detracts from the usefulness of both theories; but I am convinced that the human mind will not rest satisfied by the simple adjournment of a fundamental question of this kind.

The present work does not profess to account for the essential nature of electric charges. On the contrary, it shows that no explanation need be looked for on a scale of infinite smallness. When we get down to the electrons, we are confronted with precisely the same problem, just as the atom confronts us again with the problem of mass.

It follows that whatever advance is possible must be looked for in our own universe. Our universe is the complete epitome of sentient possibilities. It commands a distant view of the universes next below and next above in the universal scale of magnitude. Next below us we have the "infra-world," which to us appears in the shape of molecular phenomena. Next above us we have what may be called the "supra-world," which appears to us as a stellar universe, just as we appear to the inhabitants of the infra-world, if such there be.

The whole gamut of possible experiences is thus within our reach. Our physical organisation attaches us to the surface of a rolling globe, and if we ascend or descend in the scale of magnitudes we find no similar possibility of existence until the ratio becomes 10^{22} to 1. Life as we know it is confined to surfaces of planets. If there are other types of life (which is quite conceivable) they are as inaccessible to us as the inner life of a tree or a flower.

No life remotely resembling our own is possible on any scale intermediate between us and the infra-world. But if the main thesis of this essay is true, and *the infra-world is a habitable universe not essentially different from our own*, then there is no valid argument, either in physiology or psychology, to show the impossibility of our having been inhabitants of the infra-world previous to our birth into this world. A life of "seventy years" in the infra-world might be crowded with events, and yet it would add but an altogether inappreciable fraction to our earthly span of life. The facts of embryology are far from being accounted for, and the phenomena of ontogenetic development are so obscure that a reasonable hypothesis like the above can only tend towards their elucidation. It certainly removes the difficulty experienced in conceiving the boundless possibilities of life as being contained in an invisibly small germ.

Considerations such as these lend a human interest to an inquiry undertaken in the first instance for a purely physical purpose.

4. *Conditions of Life.*—How much can be done in the way of calculating conditions of existence from simple mechanical data is shown by Prof. Lowell's well-known calculation of the probable size and strength of the inhabitants of Mars. In doing the same for the infra-world, we can point to no such convincing evidence of life as the canals of Mars. Nor is that necessary for our purpose. We cannot prove that life in our sense exists in the infra-world; but we can point to its possibility, and infer its probability.

We have already seen that we can postulate an atomic structure of the "infra-world" on the plan of our own without sensibly interfering with the practical indivisibility of the atoms constituting our own world. Cohesion is 10^{22} times stronger than

with us, but the ratio of available forces to masses
is also increased 10^{22} times, so that the balance is
preserved. For forces are reduced only 10^{33} times,
while masses are reduced 10^{55} times.

Handling and moving "objects" in the infra-world
will be much the same as with us. The work per
volume will be much greater, the play of energy
more intense; but this is just what we should expect
at such a very high rate of existence. Life in the
infra-world is strenuous to an extent we little dream
of. And yet, since the means available are commen-
surate to the ends, there is no essential difference.

The span of life is proportional to the scale of time
and space. Even on our own earth there is a rough
proportionality between the length of the body of an
animal and the length of its normal span of life.
For this there is a physiological reason. Life is
essentially a succession of nerve pulses, of actions
and reactions, between the sentient self and the
external world through the medium of the physical
organism. Each such interaction consists of an
impulse travelling inwards from without, and an
answering impulse travelling outwards from within.
These impulses are transmitted by the nerves at a
certain rate depending upon certain physical properties of the transmitting substance. The rate of
transmission is comparatively slow. It is about 3000
cm. per second. Therefore, an interval of about a
tenth of a second must elapse between two succes-

sive impulses through the feet to the brain if they are to be adequately and suitably dealt with. It is just like a mercantile office in which the staff can only do business at a definite rate. This interesting physiological fact is illustrated by the coalescence of separate air-pulses into one continuous note if they exceed 40 pulses per second, and the similar coalescence of flickering images. The "central exchange" of the human machine is only constructed for some 40 exchanges per second, and it is easy to calculate that the normal span of human life contains about 10^{11} such impulses. This figure, recurring as it does again and again in our calculations, seems to be of a significance hitherto little realised. Its close proximity to the figure expressing the velocity of light in centimetres per second (3×10^{10}) is misleading, since that figure changes with the units of length and time. But another significance may attach to it independent of the units. It certainly is the *ratio* of the speed of light to the average speed of animal locomotion.

If this figure of 10^{11} (a hundred thousand million) is the allotted number of nerve-impulses for all sentient beings, it follows at once that longevity must be proportional to length. And if this is true in the infra-world, the normal span of life will be reduced 10^{22} times—*i.e.*, in the same ratio as space and time. Seventy infra-years will therefore be the normal span of life of the infra-man.

Now an infra-year is what we call a thousand billionth of a second. Hence *the lives of countless generations of beings would have time to accomplish themselves in a small fraction of our second of time.*

5. The solar system is calculated to be 1000 million years old, meaning that the planets have existed in approximately their present state and distribution for that length of time. It is estimated that they will last as long again. But even this vast span, transferred to the time scale of the infra-world, only brings us up to about a millionth of a second, or the smallest interval we can measure with our present instruments. When, therefore, we deal with molecular orbits and atomic systems, we must remember not only that we are dealing with average instantaneous values, but with average time values as well. In the shortest time taken in observing, say, the Zeeman magneto-optic effect, countless atomic systems, symbols of our own solar system, are made and unmade. Could we confine observations to a millionth of a second by a species of ultra-instantaneous photography, we might hope to observe the effect as exhibited by atomic systems as stable as our own solar system.

The stability of our own solar system is greatly increased by its distance from other fixed stars, which is over a thousand times the distance of the outermost planet. This condition is realised in the Zeeman phenomenon as observed in a sodium flame; but in solids and liquids, as R. A. Kennedy has pointed out, the conditions are essentially different. To find anything resembling them in our own universe we shall have to go to our close star clusters; but as long as the electrons we consider are in a rarefied gas, we may take it that the conditions are practically the same as in our own terrestrial world.

CHAPTER IV

INFRA-WORLD MECHANICS AND PHYSICS

1. THE physical aspect of the universe is governed
by four quantities, four "elements" of a much more
fundamental character than earth, air, fire, and
water. These four quantities are length, time,
mass, and electricity. None of these can be completely expressed by any combination of the other
three.

The conceptions of extension, space, length, area,
volume are abstractions of our own mind, which
express and embody the fundamental fact of plurality
or coexistence. There would be no need for "space"
if I were the only sentient being, and had only one
sensation at a time. I should then be quite incapable of arriving at the conception of space.
There would be nothing to suggest it. But the
simultaneous existence of beings and objects which
are independent of my will leads me to form instinctively the idea of space.

As space implies coexistence, so time implies
change. The measurement of time implies two
simultaneous changes, one of which occurs at
regular intervals—*i.e.*, intervals which are accom-

panied by the same quantity of change in many other objects.

It is well known in psychology that the eye and the touch are both at work to give the infant the sense of space. The notion of time is acquired through the eye, the ear, and the touch.

The notion of mass is more complex. It is primarily based upon the muscular sense. It involves a notion of volume and a notion of density or intensity. The observation that mere bulk does not determine the relative importance of moving objects, that two objects filling the same amount of space, and moving with the same speed, may have very different effects upon the motion of other bodies, leads to the abstraction of density, and indirectly to the idea of mass. But the idea of mass is not at all a generally familiar one. It is usually measured by weight—*i.e.*, the force exerted by the earth upon the mass. This force is proportional to the mass; but mass or inertia is quite independent of the earth and of gravitation.

Electricity is an abstraction still less familiar to untrained minds. But it is quite as fundamental as matter; indeed more so, perhaps. It involves the notion of a different kind of intensity, which is independent, within certain limits, of the quantity of matter present.

Heat is another physical quantity often measured on an independent scale. But, unlike matter and electricity, it can be generated and destroyed. Moreover, its amount can be expressed in terms of the other fundamental quantities. Therefore there is no necessity of regarding it as a fundamental quantity.

All the quantities measured in mechanics and physics are made up of measurements of one or more of the four fundamental quantities: length L, time T, mass M, and electricity E. Or if more complex quantities are measured by direct reading, as by a speed indicator or a thermometer, the result is reducible to the four fundamental quantities.

If, therefore, we wish to arrive at the mechanical and physical constitution of any imaginable universe, we have only to ascertain how its fundamental quantities compare with ours.

Thus we might postulate a world in which all masses and lengths are the same as in ours, but in which everything happens ten times as fast. Then it is easy to show that areas, volumes, angles, densities, and moments of inertia are the same as before. Acceleration, force, energy, and pressure are multiplied a hundredfold, and power a thousandfold. Velocity and angular velocity are increased ten times. But we shall be quite ignorant of any change. For our times are measured by the earth's rotation about its axis, or its revolution about the sun, and the scale of measurement increases with the quantity to be measured.

This argument applies so long as the forces involved are all purely mechanical. But it breaks down as soon as gravitational, molecular, or electric forces are brought into play. A mere increase of velocity does not increase gravitation. If the velocity of the earth increases ten times, the centrifugal force increases a hundred times, and unless gravitational force increases to the same extent, the earth will fly off into space.

We do not know what constitutes gravitational force. We only have an imperfect equation for it, viz., $F = \frac{MM^1}{D^2}$ where F is the attraction, MM^1 are the masses, and D the distance.

Gravitation is not the only force in want of a mechanical interpretation. All "actions at a distance" are in the same predicament. Coulomb's laws of electric and magnetic attraction are imperfect in their dimensions, and elasticity, cohesion, capillarity, and molecular forces generally depend upon actions which we are as yet to a great extent unfamiliar with.

If the pace of the world is accelerated, and the world is still to go on as before, all forces, mechanical, gravitational, electric, and molecular, must be increased in the same proportion—viz., as the square of the speed.

Matters are a little more complicated when not only one, but all, quantities are altered simultaneously; but the dimensional calculus again gives us a rapid method of arriving at the new quantities.

We have seen that the units of length and time are reduced 10^{22} times, thus leaving the velocities unchanged. Volumes are reduced 10^{66} times, but masses only 10^{55} times, thus implying a density 10^{11} times greater than before. Electric charges are diminished as the square root of the mass, i.e., $10^{27.5}$ times. The increase or diminution of any other physical quantity is deducible from these four, and a complete set of the physical constants of the infra-world is thus obtained by multiplying the new units in accordance with the dimensional formulæ. I append a table below. The first column gives the physical quantities, the second their dimensions, and the third the extent to which they are increased (positive index) or reduced (negative index) in the infra-world. The electrical formulæ are taken from my "Electron Theory" (p. 296).

Time	T	10^{-22}
Length	L	10^{-22}
Area	L^2	10^{-44}
Volume	L^3	10^{-66}
Angle	$A = LL^{-1}$	1
Angular velocity	AT^{-1}	10^{22}
Velocity	LT^{-1}	1
Acceleration	LT^{-2}	10^{22}
Mass	M	10^{-55}
Force	MLT^{-2}	10^{-33}
Moment	ML^2T^{-2}	10^{-55}
Work	ML^2T^{-2}	10^{-55}

Power	ML^2T^{-3}	10^{-33}
Density	ML^{-3}	10^{11}
Pressure	$ML^{-1}T^{-2}$	10^{11}
Moment of inertia	ML^2	10^{-99}
Elasticity	$ML^{-1}T^{-2}$	10^{11}
Gravitation	M^2L^{-2}	10^{-66}
Electricity	E	$10^{-27.5}$
Surface density	EL^{-2}	$10^{16.5}$
Current	ET^{-1}	$10^{-5.5}$
Electric repulsion	E^2L^{-2}	10^{-11}
Electric field	$E^{-1}MLT^{-2}$	$10^{-5.5}$
Potential	$E^{-1}ML^2T^{-2}$	$10^{-27.5}$
Capacity	$E^2M^{-1}L^{-2}T^2$	1
Resistance	$E^{-2}ML^2T^{-1}$	10^{-22}
Resistivity	$E^{-2}ML^3T^{-1}$	10^{-44}
Conductance	$E^2M^{-1}L^{-2}T$	10^{22}
Conductivity	$E^2M^{-1}L^{-3}T$	10^{44}
E.M.F.	$E^{-1}ML^2T^{-2}$	$10^{-27.5}$
Magnetic moment	EL^2T^{-1}	$10^{-49.5}$
Magnetic pole	ELT^{-1}	$10^{-27.5}$
Intensity of magnetisation . .	$EL^{-1}T^{-1}$	$10^{-16.5}$
Permeability	$E^2M^{-1}L^{-1}$	10^{22}
Inductance	$E^{-2}ML^2$	10^{-44}
Magnetic force	E^2L^{-2}	10^{-11}
Dielectric constant	$E^2M^{-1}L^{-3}T^2$	10^{22}
Magnetic field	$E^{-1}MT^{-1}$	$10^{-5.5}$
Magnetic induction	$EL^{-1}T^{-1}$	$10^{16.5}$

From this list it would be possible to compile a "Textbook of Physics for the Infra-World." The world, so constituted, has over other imaginable worlds the great advantage that it actually exists before our eyes, though on an excessively minute scale. If, therefore, we come upon any impossibilities or inconsistencies, we cannot conclude that the world cannot exist, but that there is something wrong with our deductions.

That all forces are reduced in the same proportion is evident from the fact that they balance each other. Thus, the fact that an electron can maintain its orbit for even a fraction of a second shows that for that fraction—covering millions of revolutions— its centrifugal force has been balanced by an equal and opposite attraction. If gravitation does not account for that, there must be some other force which does. That is the inevitable conclusion. Fortunately, we are acquainted with such a force in the shape of electrostatic attraction; but if we were not, we should none the less be driven to conclude that some such force existed.

Again, we see that all pressures are increased 10^{11} times, and that elasticity is increased in the same proportion. Now, elasticity is the pressure or tension required to produce a certain percentage reduction or increase in length. Pressure is force per unit area. Force is reduced 10^{33} times, but area 10^{44} times; hence pressure is increased 10^{11} times. The compression per unit length would therefore be 10^{11} times what it is with us, were it not for the fact that the density and elasticity are increased by the same amount, leaving things just as they were.

Again, a seconds pendulum in the infra-world will be 10^{22} times shorter than one in our world, and will beat infra-seconds. For its period is proportional to

$\sqrt{\frac{l}{g}}$, where l is a length and g an acceleration. The length is reduced 10^{22} times, and the acceleration, however produced, is increased 10^{22} times. Hence the quotient is reduced 10^{44} times and the periodic time 10^{22} times, thus giving infra-seconds instead of seconds.

Kinetic energy is proportional to mass, but it is more concentrated as regards volume. Infra-world bullets are much smaller than ours in proportion to their energy. Their bulk is a billion times smaller, but since all substances are correspondingly harder, they are not more penetrative than before. A remarkable reduction is that of moments of inertia, due to the simultaneous reduction of mass and length. The reduction is necessary in order to produce the proper amount of energy by rotation in a very small orbit.

In the electrical quantities, what strikes one are the comparatively enormous electric surface density and intensity of magnetisation. The latter, increased nearly a trillion times, would be the envy of our electrical engineers. Electric currents are also extremely powerful, being nearly a trillion times stronger than we could pass through the corresponding thickness of wire. But the heating effect is much less marked, as conductivity is increased 10^{44} times. Inductance is as much reduced as conductivity is increased, so that telephony ought to have made great strides in the infra-world. Both the permeability and the dielectric constant are increased 10^{22} times, *i.e.*, as much as the lengths are reduced. In the case of the latter (the "specific inductive capacity"), the increase may be interpreted as an increase in the density and mobility of the infra-electrons.

It is seen then, so far, that we can describe the physical constitution of the infra-world with considerable confidence. An attempt can also be made to arrive at some idea of the astronomical, chemical, and biological conditions prevailing there, and such an attempt shall be made in what follows.

NOTE.

Kaufmann's experiments have made it extremely probable that the whole of the mass of an electron is "electromagnetic," *i.e.*, due to the electric charge it carries. J. J. Thomson has calculated the "apparent mass" of an electron from its charge, e, and its radius, r, and finds it to be proportional to $\frac{e^2}{r}$. If m denotes the mass, we have $e^2 = mr$, a numerical coefficient being understood.

Now, if all masses were due to free electric charges, we should expect every ponderable body to be charged, and the magnitude of the charge would be expressed by $e = \sqrt{mr}$.

One charged body might revolve about another of opposite sign, the attraction being, by Coulomb's law, proportional to $\frac{ee_1}{R^2}$, or, substituting the values for e and e_1, $\frac{\sqrt{mr} \cdot \sqrt{m_1 r_1}}{R^2}$.

Now, it is easily seen (and proved by the calculus of dimensions) that if the masses m and m_1 are altered in any ratio, and the lengths rr_1 and R are altered in any other ratio, the result will always bear the same ratio to the simple fraction $\frac{m_1}{R}$.

Now, if m_1 revolves about m, the centrifugal force is $\frac{m_1 V^2}{R}$, where V is its orbital velocity. It follows immediately that if the velocity is kept constant, and the masses and distances altered in any ratio we please, the orbital motion will be maintained. For the electrostatic attraction will always change in the same ratio as the centrifugal force, and will always just balance the latter.

If the equation $e = \sqrt{mr}$ held throughout nature, with a suitable differentiation of signs, all orbital motions could be accounted for electrically. But a more probable equation is $e = D \sqrt{mr}$, where D is the average " world density."

CHAPTER V

INFRA-ASTRONOMY

1. It has been shown, so far, that the world of atoms and electrons is a world which is physically and mechanically not essentially different from ours, its chief distinctions being the substitution of electrical for gravitational attraction, and the much greater densities, pressures, and elasticities prevailing in the infra-world.

Our attention must be now directed to what may be called the astronomy of the infra-world. And since astronomy is a large-scale science, we shall find many links between the infra-world and our own world. These links are due to the remarkable circumstance that (always supposing the infra-world to be inhabited by beings like ourselves), *the largest object visible in the infra-world is one of the smallest visible objects of our own world.* In other words, the "starry heavens" of the infra-world appear to us as a minute microscopic speck.

But the minute specks visible to us have very diverse constitutions, densities, and chemical, physical, and biological properties, and the chances are that none of them correspond in structure to our visible universe. As a matter of fact, our visible universe resembles a rarefied gas rather than a liquid or solid. For the average distance between the molecules of atmospheric air is 1000 times their diameter, whereas the distance of the nearest fixed star is 3000 times the diameter of the solar system, and the other stars are much further off. Other parts of our universe are, of course, much denser, and approach more closely to what we may call the liquid state. But the starry universe immediately surrounding us corresponds to a gas, with solar systems for molecules.

For a solid like a copper wire we have no analogy on our own world scale. For the atoms of copper are so densely packed as to be in actual contact, or even compressed. If we brought the stars of the Milky Way into actual contact, there would inevitably be a great conflagration, in the course of which their individuality would be hopelessly lost. There is less chance of that in the infra-world, since the hardness of the bodies is much greater, while the velocities remain the same. But there is another circumstance which enables the atoms—the solar system of the infra-world—to approach each other as far as the orbits of their outermost electrons and yet remain separate systems. It is the electrostatic repulsion between the electrons thus brought close together. Most atoms have a large number of electrons revolving round them, estimated in some cases at several hundred or even thousand, though only two or three of these are ever detached from them. They revolve in all kinds of orbits with various planes, and not in the same direction, except in the case of the magnetic substances. Their charges are neutralised by the positive charge of the central atom, so that at considerable distances they exert no electrostatic action. They may still, however, exert a magnetic action. For if the electrons revolve in the same sense, they constitute a molecular magnet, which attracts or repels similar systems, and may strengthen or oppose the gravitational attraction between them. But when two such systems come close together, the electrons, being outermost, act upon each other with the well-known electrostatic repulsion. All molecular phenomena point clearly to an attraction between atoms which gives way to a repulsion at close quarters, and an explanation of this rule, although beset with many difficulties, must be looked for in some such line of reasoning.

The atoms will take up positions of equilibrium dictated by their gravitational and magnetic attraction and electrostatic repulsion. The systems of equilibrium will obviously depend upon the number of electrons and their orbits, and will vary from one species of atoms to another. The para-magnetic atoms, or those whose electrons revolve in an ecliptic plane like our planets, will form lines or closed chains in obedience to their magnetic attraction.

These chains will make the structure of the magnetic elements more complex than that of non-magnetic elements.

When two atoms come into contact without being crowded by others, as, for instance, in a gas, it may well happen that one of the electrons gets detached from one atom and describes an orbit round the other. It is just as if a Centauri, for instance, were close enough to our solar system to capture Neptune. With a suitable speed, the two solar systems would combine and revolve about each other, and our system would become a double star like most of the other visible stars.

2. Now, imagine two neutral atoms in the infra-world. To the infra-man they appear as stars or suns, not necessarily single spheres, like our sun, but possibly larger aggregations of such spheres, like heaps of cannon-balls, prevented from coalescing by their strong cohesion and great hardness. Each of these suns, whether simple or composite, is surrounded by electrons revolving in all directions as irregular as the satellites of Uranus or the new satellite of Saturn. The total charge of the electrons is neutralised by the positive charge of the central body, so that any single electron, removed some distance from the system, is subjected to an attraction equal to the repulsion between two electrons at the same distance. The system from which the electron is removed becomes what is called a "positive atom." If, on

the other hand, a new electron (or "infra-planet")
is added to the system, the latter becomes a "negative
atom." It is obvious that only those electrons will
be liable to loss which have either very large or very
eccentric orbits, and as a rule the same atom cannot
lose more than two or three at the most.

Two such atomic systems, then, approach each other
so closely that one electron is transferred from one
system to another. This transfer immediately sets up
an electrostatic attraction between the two systems,
equal to the attraction between a single electron and
a single positive atom. The future behaviour of the
two systems will depend upon their original speed.
If that is excessive, they will fly apart again—no
longer as neutral atoms, but one of them a positive
atom and the other a negative atom. But if the
speed is moderate, they will revolve round each
other and form a binary. Needless to say, the
revolutions will be much slower than the revolution
of electrons in their orbits, both on account of the
greater distance apart and the greater mass of the
revolving bodies. Unlike our astronomy, the infra-
astronomy is obliged to acknowledge a dependence
of the rate of revolution upon the mass of the revolving body, since the force is mainly electrical, and
is not proportional to the masses, but to the charges.

After the transfer, the probabilities are that the
captured electron becomes an "inferior planet" in
the capturing system, so that it runs no risk of

being recaptured. The infra-man therefore has the gorgeous spectacle of two suns majestically revolving round each other, each attended with its planets, one of them being transferred from one system to another as a pledge of union.

The above process is what happens in the formation of, say, a hydrogen molecule. The molecule is really a binary star consisting of two atoms linked by electrostatic force. If the speed of encounter is excessive the result is two free-flying atoms, one with a positive and the other with a negative elementary charge. Needless to say, when two such atoms meet again their union is considerably facilitated by their electrostatic attraction.

When from any cause the molecule is split up, each atom will take its own electrons away with it, and the atoms will constitute what is called "nascent hydrogen." It is easily seen that the latter must possess more pronounced combining properties than neutral hydrogen. The splitting-up of molecules into charged atomic systems is called ionisation. Such ionisation may be brought about not only by collision, but by a number of other agencies, such as Röntgen rays, or ultra-violet light. There are probably also cases of what may be called spontaneous ionisation, brought about as follows :—

The superior or outer electrons of each system revolve under the attraction of the central positive body. They undergo perturbations by the other

D

electrons, which periodically subject them to a
greater repulsion as they approach them in what
we call "conjunction." As a general rule, these
perturbations, like those in the solar system, are
not serious, being outweighed by the much greater
attraction of the central body, and also, to some
extent, by the electrodynamic ("magnetic") attraction between the moving electrons. But every now
and then it will happen that a larger number of
electrons are in conjunction together, and then the
outermost ones will stand in danger of being expelled
from their orbits and set roaming at large. The
likelihood of such a contingency happening depends,
of course, upon a variety of circumstances, such as
the structure and size of the central body, the distribution and number of the electrons, &c. It may
well happen that as the central body increases in
mass the likelihood of expulsion oscillates between
a number of maxima and minima. At the minima
the system would have the greatest ability to take up
an extra electron; but this process would be much
rarer than the loss of electrons, owing to the repulsion of the other electrons which would have to
be overcome. In short, it is much easier for a
neutral system to lose an electron than to acquire
an extra one.

Here we have, then, something like an explanation
of the Periodic Law in its electro-chemical aspect.
As we proceed from lower to higher atomic weights,

the elements become alternately electro-positive (liable to lose one or more electrons) and electro-negative (able to take up an additional electron). The former are more numerous than the latter.

Both kinds of atoms are, of course, liable to both loss and gain of electrons. Thus chlorine, which gains an electron easily, is just as well able to form molecules as hydrogen, which loses them easily. But when chlorine molecules and hydrogen molecules meet, the positive hydrogen atom quickly joins the negative chlorine atom, while the negative hydrogen atom as quickly passes its superfluous electron over to the positive chlorine atom, and then loses another electron to it. The union between the two hydrogen and the two chlorine atoms is thus dissolved, and two molecules of hydrochloric acid are formed instead of the original molecules. This change, which liberates a considerable potential energy, gives rise to a great speed of translation or rotation of the combining bodies, which to us appears as heat.

To give a more graphic picture of these occurrences than can be obtained by a technical description, we may put them into the form of a chronicle of an infra-world observatory situated, say, on an electron which we will call Talav,[1] revolving round a hydrogen atom named Grean,[1] contained in a gas containing other hydrogen and chlorine atoms. Talav is an

[1] These names are the Irish equivalents of "earth" and "sun."

inner planet of Grean. The outer planets are called Prima, Secunda, and Tertia, in order of distance. The other stars are called Alpha, Beta, &c.

3. *From the Records of the Talav Observatory.*

Year 5280, *July* 1.—This year's conjunction of Prima, Secunda, and Tertia is looked forward to with considerable interest. Tertia will certainly be lost to our system if she undergoes any additional outward perturbation.

Oct. 5.—Last night's observations show that the conjunction has not expelled Tertia. She is therefore safe for another 72 years, unless something extraordinary happens.

Year 5283, *Feb.* 5.—An unknown comet has been sighted in the orbital plane of Secunda. Approaching with a speed of 10^8 cm. per second, and will pass Grean at half Talav's distance. Will probably join our system.

March 1.—New comet turns out to be a planet of the size and mass of Talav, and same charge. Has joined our system, and will have an orbit of great eccentricity, extending considerably beyond that of Tertia.

Year 5285, *March* 15.—New planet is approaching apo-Grean, but is showing decided perturbations, which are shared by all other planets. These are cosmic and periodic. Period estimated at three months.

April 4.—New planet's orbit has become parabolic under influence of cosmic perturbations, and the planet will be lost to our system.

(*Terrestrial Note.*—The above entries represent a case of ionisation by ultra-violet light.)

Year 5352, *June* 16.—The approaching conjunction is expected to pass off without unusual developments, in spite of the cosmic perturbations, which are too feeble to affect Tertia's orbit.

Nov. 5.—A pulse of unusual strength travelled through our system to-day. It was first detected at 9.15 A.M., when Tertia began to show a considerable acceleration. At noon a similar acceleration was observed in Secunda, and Prima, now in opposition, showed a retardation, first discovered at 4 P.M. The pulse lasted for about half-an-hour.

Nov. 6.—Two more pulses travelled through our system to-day, one beginning at 2 A.M. and the other at 4.30 A.M.

Nov. 7.—Four more pulses to-day, one in the morning and three in the afternoon. The pulses are now ascribed to collisions of the New Planet of 5285 with the system of Gamma, which is approaching.

Nov. 10.—Tertia appears to be definitely lost. The pulses at conjunction sufficed to make her orbit hyperbolic.

Year 5362, *July* 15.—Tertia has dwindled to a star of 12th magnitude. Gamma is approaching at a speed of about 10^4 cm. per second.

(*Terrestrial Note.*—The above entries represent a case of ionisation by Röntgen rays.)

Year 5365, *March* 3.—Much interest has been aroused by the observation that the motion of Gamma shows a perceptible acceleration, directed towards our system. A corresponding acceleration of the motion of Grean has been proved to exist by numerous fixed-star observations.

June 12.—The acceleration of the proper motions of Grean and Gamma greatly exceeds that attributable to gravitation. It is now supposed that Gamma has acquired an extra planet, thus giving it a negative charge sufficient to account for the force.

Year 5366, *Aug.* 1.—Gamma is now seen to show a perceptible disc. Its distance is estimated at 10^{18} cm.

Sept. 15.—Gamma is now seen as a large star with at least two outer planets. The innermost of these is retrograde, with considerable eccentricity. It has been provisionally identified with the new planet of 5285.

Year 5367, *April* 30.—There is every likelihood of our being converted into a binary. The elements of Gamma indicate an elliptic orbit round our common centre of gravity.

Aug. 25.—Gamma is now fully visible with the naked eye as a sun one-tenth the diameter of Grean. The two are now in opposition, and there is per-

petual day. The period of our common revolution
is estimated at 1135 years.

(*Terrestrial Note.*—The above entries represent
the formation of a hydrogen molecule from a
positive atom — Grean, and a negative atom —
Gamma.)

Year 5830, *Jan.* 10.—A large number of new
stars appeared last night near the pole of the
Ecliptic. Before dawn 86 were counted. Spectroscopic observations indicate a speed of 10^{10} cm.
per second.

Jan. 11, 3 P.M.—One of the new stars just passed
Talav within ten diameters, producing considerable
tidal action. The velocity of the body was enormous,
the passage from horizon to horizon occupying only
a quarter of an hour.

4 P.M.—Gamma has been struck by two of the
shooting stars. The system of Gamma shows considerable perturbation.

Jan. 12, *midnight.*—Twelve more bodies have
passed. It is impossible to calculate their probable
effect at present. The bodies are planets of mass,
diameter, and charge same as Talav.

March 15.—The phenomenal invasion of planets
of January last has had the effect of dissolving our
binary. Gamma is moving away with speed sufficient to remove it from Grean's influence. Our
system is still short by one planet, thus giving it
an elementary positive charge.

(*Terrestrial Note.*—The above entries represent a case of ionisation by cathode rays.)

4. This sketch represents, as closely as we know it, the actual appearances which would be presented to an observer reduced to a size comparable with an electron instead of the earth, who measured his times by the revolutions of his electrons instead of the revolutions of the earth. The events which to us are crowded into a billionth of a second would then appear to occupy several hours, and the tremendous and far-reaching chemical and physical changes would be spread over very long intervals of time, making them practically of as little influence to the daily life of the infra-men as the proper motions of the stars are to us.

CHAPTER VI

OPTICS, CHEMISTRY, AND BIOLOGY
OF THE INFRA-WORLD

1. IN order to arrive at some idea of the chemical structure of the planets of the infra-world on the basis of the general considerations advanced in Chapter IV., we must carry the fundamental analogies to their logical conclusion. We have seen that in both our world and the infra-world velocities are of the same order of magnitude, while lengths are reduced in the ratio of $10^{22} : 1$. We have also taken it for granted that the infra-world has an atomic constitution—an assumption which must hold the field until some other constitution will have been proved to be thinkable. Given this atomic constitution, there will be an infra-chemistry as well as an infra-astronomy. But chemistry not only requires atoms, but electrons as well. In fact, the familiar machinery of chemistry (now practically resolved into electricity and thermo-dynamics) must be there in all its essential features. The ether being unchanged, the motions of the infra-electrons will produce ether-waves — otherwise light — and, to complete the analogy, the

wave-length of this light must on the average be 10^{22} times smaller than the light visible to our own eyes. The velocity of propagation being the same as that of our light, the number of revolutions per second for the infra-electrons must be 10^{22} times that of the electrons, and 10^{14} times that of our earth. What mechanism will be necessary for such a rate of revolution?

The dimensional calculus will again enable us to solve this problem at a glance. Suppose that the fundamental quantities M, L, T, and E are changed over again in the same ratio as before. They will now become 10^{-110}, 10^{-44}, 10^{-44}, and 10^{-55} times what they are in our world. But the table on p. 39 shows that electrostatic attraction and centrifugal force will no longer balance each other, since the latter is again reduced to 10^{-33} and the former only to 10^{-11}. In other words, the electric attraction between an infra-atom and its attendant infra-electron will be 10^{22} times too great to balance the centrifugal force. Hence there will be no separation between atoms and electrons, and no light or chemical action.

Now we have a choice between two alternatives. Either we assume that the infra-infra-world bears the same relation to the infra-world as the latter does to our world, in which case, as we have seen, no infra-light is possible, and the infra-world is dark; or we assume that electric charges are not influenced by the average density of the bodies beyond a certain density. To understand the significance of the latter assumption we must return to p. 43, where the electric charge of a body is expressed by $e = D \sqrt{mr}$, and D is the average density of the universe in question, m is the mass, and r the radius of a planetary body in it. The D was introduced in order to bring the electric charge of an electron up to a point sufficient to replace gravitational attraction. But Maxwell's original equation for the relation between mass and charge is $m = \frac{e^2}{r}$, or $e = \sqrt{mr}$. If this equation holds good for the infra-electron, its charge will be $10^{-38 \cdot 5}$ that of an electron instead of $10^{-27 \cdot 5}$, and the electrostatic attraction will be reduced 10^{33} times— *i.e., in the same proportion as the centrifugal force.* Therefore the electric force will balance the centrifugal force, as in the infra-world, and luminous vibrations and chemical action are possible.

The light of the infra-world, like any other transverse ether disturbance, will have a velocity of 3×10^{10} cm. per second. It will, therefore, pass out of the atomic system in something like a trillionth of a second. But since the scale of time is also reduced, the same passage will take 10,000 infra-seconds, or something under three infra-hours. The velocity of light will, therefore, play the same part in the infra-world as it does in our world.

An interesting question now arises as to what part the light of the infra-world plays in our world : Can we see it, or tell its existence in any way ? The answer is, that infra-light is extreme ultra-violet light, and quite beyond our means of measurement. We possess no instrument capable of directly indicating infra-light, even if it exists. But its indirect effects are not beyond hope of discovery. Light is known to exert a perceptible effect upon comets' tails. If infra-light exerts an effect upon the motion of electrons, it may, at some future time, become possible to trace such effect. The most likely substances to show such an effect are the radio-active bodies, and it will be remembered that Professor and Madame Curie assumed the existence of some such radiation to account for the energy of radium.

Although infra-light is extremely feeble, it must be remembered that if it is emitted by infra-electrons it must be emitted by the whole visible universe. For the visible universe is co-extensive with the infra-world. The latter is a world within a world. To explore the infra-world instead of this world is something like drawing the plan of a house instead of a map of the terrestrial globe.

Sunlight may contain infra-light as one of its constituents. But since light is only absorbed by electrons having a period akin to its own, infra-light is only absorbed by infra-electrons, and its effect on the whole electron is likely to remain undiscoverable.

Here, then, we have a remarkable result. The world may be blazing with a powerful light quite inaccessible to our present senses, and quite un-discoverable to our instruments, and yet it may (unlike extreme ultra-violet light as hitherto known) have a whole world of responsive substances to act upon. This light will make up a considerable portion of the energy passing through the ether, and we may never be able to detect it. Yet it is absorbed by matter (by infra-electrons, in fact); but the effects of such absorption are internal, and are embodied in small-scale phenomena in the infra-world, just as sunlight is absorbed by the earth without perceptibly affecting its annual period of revolution.

2. *Infra-Chemistry.*—It is a mistake to suppose that the enormous density of the objects of the infra-world—10^{11} times that of water—precludes the happening of the ordinary physical and chemical events known to us. Liquid and gaseous states are quite as possible there as they are in our world. A solid state implies that the atoms are so closely packed as to admit no displacement among each other. In a liquid state this structure is loosened to such an extent that the atoms are rarely out of each other's range of gravitational attraction, but still are free to change their grouping. A gaseous

state implies a lack of density such that atoms are most of the time beyond gravitational range—*i.e.*, that their motions are not sensibly affected by gravitational attraction.

The existence of these states depends in the main upon "temperature," or mean kinetic energy. Now, a greatly-increased density, such as we have in the infra-world, means a greatly-increased cohesion. It does not mean that a larger proportion of the space occupied by a body is occupied by its material substance, and a smaller proportion by the ether. We have, indeed, supposed all along that the proportion is the same as in our world (reckoning atoms and electrons as "solid"). It simply means that the particles constituting the atom or electron are 10^{11} times denser than the atoms or electrons themselves, just as these, again, are denser than the earth or sun.

The increased cohesion, while giving the electron the necessary power of resisting disintegration by electric forces, is incapable of maintaining the material of the electron in a permanently solid state. For the same density that brings about the increased cohesion also brings about an increase of mean kinetic energy, otherwise temperature. Hence, the "seas" on the surface of the electron can be liquid although of extreme specific gravity.

Most chemical actions we know of occur in the liquid state. Given the three states of aggregation, a suitable temperature, and powerful electric forces, we only require differences of elementary substance in order to have what we call chemical action.

Differences of substance imply, as we know, differences of atomic weight. Taking the atomic weight as the sole criterion of elementary substance, we find less than a hundred elementary substances in our world. There is at present no evidence that the stars are graduated in a definite series of increasing weights. If they were, and we could determine their weights, we might, putting stars for atoms, make out how many "substances" constitute the supra-world. If there is an infinite gradation of weights, and no corresponding planetary or electrical difference between the various stars, we must conclude that there is no "supra-chemistry." In our present ignorance on this point, we cannot judge by analogy as to the substances, consisting of infra-atoms, which constitute the infra-world. But if there is a much greater specialisation of matter in our world than in the supra-world, we may take it that the chemical substances of the infra-world are better defined than ours, and fewer in number, with larger gaps between successive atomic weights. This would give the infra-atoms that greater stability which would be necessary to resist the further increase of electric disintegrating force and the greater energy of chemical reaction.

This greater energy is on a par with the greater electric actions, and with the pace of events generally in the infra-world. Relatively, however, there is no essential difference between infra-chemical phenomena and the chemical phenomena of this world.

3. *Infra-Biology.*—Given a requisite amount and kind of mechanical, electrical, thermal, and chemical action, an infra-physiological activity looms into the realm of the possible. The fewness of the chemical elements is no bar to infra-biology, since the elements essential to life are comparatively few—five or six out of nearly a hundred.

Our actual evidence of material life is limited to a thin and precarious crust of a single planet, or two planets, Earth and Mars, at the most. There is, of course, nothing to prove that "dead matter" may not be endowed with some kind of rudimentary consciousness. We can certainly distinguish both a rudimentary fatigue and a rudimentary formation of habit in inorganic substances, both phenomena which indicate something of the nature of memory. Dr. Bose goes so far as to trace what he calls a response to stimulus in metals. But physiological life, properly so called, involves a set of changes and adaptations which are clearly marked off from the changes occurring in dead matter, and which are invariably accompanied—if not conditioned —by the presence of certain carbon and nitrogen compounds of remarkable instability. When, in any aggregation of solid and liquid matter, these compounds are continually formed and destroyed, and when the energy thus liberated is directed towards increasing this metabolism and making it more permanent, we diagnose the presence of organic life.

Perhaps the nearest physical counterpart to an organism is a flame. In a flame there is a definite chemical change going on whose effect is directed towards its own stability, and is derived from the energy liberated in the change. There is also a constant change of the matter constituting the flame, and even a differentiation of parts, combustible matter being taken in and mixed with oxygen below, and products of combustion being eliminated above. There is also growth to a maximum depending on the conditions of "nutrition." There is death when the nutrition falls below a certain minimum. Flames are capable both of union and fission, and the latter is indeed the common method of propagation. As regards the supply of energy and the final products of its transformation, the flame resembles the animal rather than the vegetable kingdom. But the analogy can be carried much further, though in doing so it tends to become more and more superficial. Thus, in lighting a candle we strike a match. The head of the match is the germ which at a certain temperature bursts into life, and that life feeds for some time on the stick. On being

E

transferred to the wick, the flame descends in its
search for food, and develops to its full size when
it has secured an adequate supply. It can be
"killed" by destroying its most vital organ—the
part where the solid food is converted into gas.
Many flames are "sensitive" to particular sounds.
Some even develop a "protective covering," as in a
smouldering fire.

The analogy is so far-reaching that we might
describe a flame as a *gaseous non-centralised
animal* were it not for the total absence of anything resembling habit or memory. Thus a sensitive flame will respond to the same stimulus in
the same manner, no matter how often it is applied.
It might be urged that the life of a flame is so
"strenuous" that the intervals between successive
stimuli would have to be excessively short; but
this is refuted by the stroboscopic study of responsive flames, which shows a practically instantaneous and uniform response.

The flame has no cellular structure, and therefore no organisation. Even if it is regarded as
consisting of a single cell, it differs from the
amœba in possessing no nucleus. Since the fission
or fusion of nuclei is the essential feature of all
animal reproduction and propagation, we are bound
to regard the nucleus as the repository of the
animal's "experience," ready to hand it on to
posterity. The simultaneous absence of memory

and of a nucleus in a flame then becomes intelligible.

The above considerations will help us to solve the question of life in the infra-world. We have already seen that there is no reason to postulate the absence of any of the three states of aggregation of matter known to us. There is plenty of light and heat in all probability. The conditions of organic life are all present, and as regards geological time, the infra-world has much more of that than we have, since what is a second in our world is a thousand billion years in the infra-world. There is, therefore, plenty of time for organic evolution, and, indeed, for an evolution which transcends all our present conceptions of its possibilities. Yet a simple consideration will show that the evolution of the infra-world has well-defined limits. As far as we can judge, the infra-world is always the same in its physical properties. Whatever evolution is in progress there does not affect those properties of the infra-world which we are able to gauge, such as the constancy of the elementary atoms and electrons. Our historical records go back some 8000 years, which is 80 quadrillion infra-years, and in all that immense time the "evolution" of the infra-world has not sufficed to change its apparent properties. Transferring this analogy to our own world, it would mean that for an almost inconceivable span of future time organic life in our world, however highly developed, will not be able to produce new results on an astronomical scale, or to affect the motion of heavenly bodies.

The same analogy gives us a new conception of the permanence of our own universe. During the last century we have been, unknown to ourselves, surveying and examining the properties of the infra-world over a period of a quadrillion infra-years. They show no sign of variation, although the chances of such variation are as great as the chances our world would get in a quadrillion of our years. But this argument can be logically extended into infinity. For an inhabitant of the infra-world can, in a period of 100 infra-years, make the same statement concerning the next lower world (which we might call the infra^2-world), any essential change of which would react upon the superior world it constitutes. *The constancy of natural laws is, therefore, an objective proof of the infinite duration and stability of our universe.*

4. It is a curious—though somewhat idle—calculation to determine the number of electrons contained in the adult human body. It is about 10^{31}. Now, the earth contains at least 1,000,000,000 (10^9) human beings, not to mention other living beings. Therefore, the number of infra-men which we can accommodate in our own bodies figures out at about 10^{40}. And yet the total activity of all these

beings, for untold infra-geological eras, is without the slightest net effect on our own consciousness.

This calculation, though doubtful in a quantitative sense, brings home to us the fact that our consciousness is mercifully protected from the teeming life of matter, just as it is largely unaware of the multiform organic processes which go on in the life of each constituent cell of the human body. Our mind resembles the Registrar-General in a census. The census officers penetrate into every remote hamlet, and every house, and before the figures reach the Registrar-General they have been summed up and boiled down by a large staff of intermediate officials. The Registrar-General gets the net result. He may do the same amount of work as his subordinates—I shall charitably suppose that he does—but he surveys the country as a whole, and a unit more or less is indifferent to him. In the same way, our consciousness, or at least our normal consciousness, is not lost in detail, however complex that may be. There is a summarising and integrating power within us which is constantly at work, and which adjusts external events to a scale within our purview. Hence the revelation of the infinite complexity of matter need not overwhelm us with a hopeless sense of tangle and complication. This world is an intelligible world to an almost infinite extent. We are understanding it more and more fully. The advance of science leads to simpler and fewer formulæ, just as the advance of civilisation simplifies the satisfaction of our elementary needs. Every new natural law discovered registers a vast array of facts automatically in order. The outstanding puzzles largely concern the infinite and the infinitesimal. It has often been supposed that these two regions are beyond the grasp of the human intellect. But that has been shown to be fallacious ever since the discovery of the infinitesimal calculus.

The infra-world is not an infinitesimal world, except in a relative sense. It can be dealt with on a finite scale, just as a differential coefficient can, and a succession of infinitesimals and infinitudes of several orders can be dealt with according to recognised algebraic principles. This indicates the possibility of bringing the whole chain of universes within the purview of our present-day science.

CHAPTER VII

MATTER AND LIFE FROM WITHIN

1. OUR investigations up to this have given many
reasons for believing, and none for disbelieving, that
a world resembling the universe known to us exists
around us on a very much smaller, but not infinitely
smaller, scale. We have seen, in fact, that it is
possible for two similar universes, differing only in
the size of its discrete particles, to occupy the same
space at the same time. Also, that to leave one
universe and enter another, it is only necessary
that our size be reduced or increased 10^{22} times,
or the ratio of the sizes of the starry heavens and
the smallest visible speck of dust. Events happen in
the small-scale universe, the infra-world, as much
more rapidly as its sizes are smaller.

There is an ancient Irish legend about a land
called Tir nan-Ogue, the Land of the Young. Those
who, like Ossian, spent what they thought were
three years there, found on their return to Ireland
that three centuries had passed by during their
absence in the Field of Bliss. This is the converse
of a visit to the infra-world. Such a visit would resemble more closely our usual experience in dreams,

where a long and complicated course of events is crowded into a fraction of a second.

An Inner View of Matter.—In the chapter on Infra-Astronomy, I sketched out the actual appearance of the infra-world as seen within a rarefied gas, and illustrated the various phenomena of "ionisation" by astronomical analogies. There is every reason for believing that the atoms and molecules of a rarefied gas appear to inhabitants of the infra-world very much like what the starry heavens appear to us. But when we consider the aspect of the infra-world as presented with a solid or liquid instead of a rarefied gas, we come to aspects with which we cannot trace any analogy in our own world. What would be, for instance, the internal appearance of a copper wire, or a crystal of calcspar, or a piece of ice? In endeavouring to get at the solution of this difficult question, we must first of all obtain some insight into the constitution of the "positive atom." We find by chemical experiment that all known substances may be arranged in a series of weights marking their atoms and determining most of their properties. The series begins with hydrogen, whose atomic weight is arbitrarily called unity, and ends with uranium, with an atomic weight of 240 units. It is found that the physical, chemical, and electrical properties of the elements change in regular periods as the atomic weight increases. Elements of the same general properties are found by adding 16, 32, or 48 units to the atomic weight of any given body.

Now this is a state of things for which we can trace no parallel in our world. That may possibly be because we cannot deal with our stars on a scale of sufficient magnitude to survey them as we survey atoms. But so far as we can survey the starry universe, there is no definite and step-by-step gradation of stars according to their masses. That such a gradation does exist in the infra-world we must put down to the greater power of the electric forces at work there.

Why more matter should be associated with positive electricity than with negative is one of those ultimate questions for which we have as yet no solution whatever. Why is the smallest " positive atom "—that of hydrogen—more than a thousand times heavier than the electron? Why are there no positive electrons? It has been suggested that electrons are permanent sources of ether, and positive atoms permanent sinks of ether, the ether welling out of transcendental space in the one case, and being drained back into the same space in the other. Such an " explanation " would account for the dissimilarity observed ; but I prefer not to have recourse to " transcendental " conceptions, which may, or may not, have a meaning. Once we admit that in any universe, however minute its scale, positive electricity is associated with more matter than negative, it is comparatively easy to account for a like distribution in any higher universe. Take the example of the sun. Why has the sun a positive charge, and the earth a negative charge? Simply because the sun emits a more powerful radiation, which has a repulsive action on finely divided matter, such as the droplets condensed about electrons. The sun, therefore, is constantly expelling negative electricity until its own charge suffices to maintain the equilibrium between emission and absorption.

We need only postulate that as we descend to the infra-world, the radiation of the positive central bodies decreases more slowly than the mass in order to account for the much greater intensity of the electric charges. In fact, we must suppose that the "infra-light" emitted by the atoms is much more powerful in comparison with their size, than the light emitted by the sun. Tentatively, we might suppose that the radiation varies, not as the mass, but as the square root of the mass.

This would give us, then, our positively-charged atom or infra-star. Now there are reasons for assuming that the hydrogen-atom is not only the arbitrary unit of atomic weight, but a real and ultimate physical unit of the same importance as the electron. This is Prout's hypothesis, which has not been strictly verified, but which may yet receive a new interpretation when the mass of the electrons bound up with the atoms is allowed for. In any case, the phenomena of radio-activity have made it very probable that the heavier atoms—such as those of uranium and radium—break up by expelling helium atoms. These may or may not have been in a state of chemical "combination" with them. In these matters we must avoid using such a word pedantically. It is enough that the helium atom escapes somehow. Now the atomic weight of helium is 4. It most likely consists of four hydrogen atoms. How can these be so combined?

If, as we have assumed, the positive atoms have a charge equal to that of one or more electrons, surely they will fly asunder! But here we may well have a converse case from that of neutral atoms in contact. Positive atoms are heavier than electrons. Their gravitational attraction is greater in comparison with their charge. Therefore, although electrons may be mutually repulsive to such an enormous extent that they never come into actual contact, this may not be so with positive atoms. And if they do happen to touch, it is possible that their adhesion may suffice to overcome their mutual electric repulsion, just as in a former case the gravitational attraction of two neutral atoms with their attendant swarms of electrons was balanced by the repulsion of the latter.

Now it is easy to show that the simplest structure of perfect stability that can thus be built up out of hydrogen atoms contains four atoms, forming a tetrahedron or equilateral pyramid. Such a structure we may identify with the helium atom.

Larger atoms are built up out of larger aggregates of hydrogen atoms, and the manner of their architecture is one of the most fascinating problems awaiting the coming electric theory of crystals. But we may well suppose that the helium atom never loses its stability and predominance. It is interesting to note that similar elements in the periodic series are made up by adding 16, 32, or 48 hydrogen units to the atomic weight; in other words, by adding four, eight, or twelve helium atoms. These are probably disposed symmetrically, on the principle of the tetrahedron, the octahedron, and the dodecahedron. When the atom breaks up these projecting helium atoms are the first to be thrown off, as is done when radium and polonium atoms break up.

2. It would be an interesting task to endeavour to follow up the influence of the configuration of the compound atoms and their attendant electrons on the building up of a crystalline or amorphous solid. It will, no doubt, be a long time before a complete mathematical theory is formulated which accounts for the delicate balancing of the hydrogen atoms within the positive atom and the molecules within the crystal. The researches already made

into the structure of compounds by the methods
of stereo-chemistry offer a solid foundation for
work along this line. But imagine a molecule of,
say, quinine, consisting of twenty atoms of carbon,
twenty-four of hydrogen, two of nitrogen, and two
of oxygen, arranged in groups and sub-groups, the
whole molecule a veritable phalanx of stars, the
suns swaying in gentle oscillations or slow orbits,
the planets darting round as if to preserve the
integrity of the empire of their central luminary,
the whole system ablaze with light and astir with
motion, a piece of stellar architecture besides
which Orion is without form and void; and this
molecule built into a gorgeous system of a trillion
units of like structure, all of which go to make up
a single grain of the crystalline powder we know to
be the invaluable antidote to the fevers of the
tropical forest.

A somewhat less imposing spectacle would be
presented to an infra-man who takes his stand on
an electron inside a copper wire, and waits till the
current was turned on. The sky would not only
be ablaze with stars, he would be surrounded on
all sides with suns, and his electron would be at
a loss to know to which sun it owned allegiance.
It would revolve for a thousand infra-years, perhaps,
round one particular copper atom; then it would
spend two or three months running free, and would
eventually be drawn into the power of another of

those "mighty atoms," to pass another thousand years in thraldom. When the switch is turned in our world, a new cycle of evolution begins among the atoms of the wire. The infra-man finds a new force and purpose at work among the roving infra-planets. Whenever they are free, they all tend to move towards one particular part of the sky, being driven by the push of other infra-planets intruded into the system from behind. While the infra-suns (atoms) keep fairly well within their allotted spaces, the electrons find their way down the slope of potential, threading their way among the atoms by fits and starts, and making up what we call the electron current or negative current.

3. *Life from Within.* — We have no reason to believe that organic matter, such as protoplasm, has a structure essentially different from inorganic matter. There is no doubt less stability, less definiteness of structure, a more rapid transformation of molecules, a continual binding and unbinding of electrons. There is, in short, more chaos than cosmos. It is just as if chemical transformations in organised matter were too multifarious and rapid to allow any part of it to settle down to a definite chemical composition. Those portions which are most alive show the greatest chemical instability, the greatest lack of definite chemical properties. Carbon and nitrogen, two elements

distinguished for their variety of linkages, play the most essential part in organised matter. The albuminous colloids, whose composition has hitherto defied definition, consist of some 53 parts of carbon, 16 parts of nitrogen, 20 of oxygen, 7 of hydrogen, and 1 of sulphur. A single molecule of any definite substance made up out of these would be lost in the welter of nebulous and disaggregated matter, and could not be detected by our analyses. A living cell from within would therefore appear like an utterly unsystematic congeries of atoms, molecules, and ruins of molecules more or less complex. The atoms, or infra-suns, would be of six or seven different types, and none of them exceptionally large. A human brain cell would perhaps be the most chaotic of all, the atoms undergoing a rapid series of groupings and rearrangements, every such grouping being the physical symbol and counterpart of a conscious or subconscious thought.

This brings us to some problems of existence which have long been very obscure, but which appear less so when regarded in the light of the infra-world. We have, in all our investigations, found no point at which a final continuity and unity can be demonstrated. Everything is divisible, infinitely divisible, and, however deeply we descend in the scale of magnitude, the whirl of atoms and the drift of suns remains the same.

Where, then, is that "unifying principle" upon which we have relied to preserve our minds from the intolerable complexity of the universe?

That such a question should be asked at all shows how a mechanical view of natural phenomena has obscured our appreciation of the realities underlying all human understanding. Atoms, electrons, material objects generally are not realities. They are *our* conceptions of realities which affect our sensorium, constructed in our minds from material supplied by our past experiences. Our experiences are the only realities of which we have definite evidence, and these are finally resolvable into sensations and memories of sensations. By an act of faith we extend our own sphere of sensation to include spheres which we perceive to be similar, and we thus are enabled to see with other persons' eyes and remember with other persons' memories. By another act of faith we postulate an "object" behind a bundle of permanent or recurring sensations. These sensations are the symbol of that object, the signs by which it reveals its presence to us. No doubt the object contains some ultimate reality, but what that ultimate reality may be, what the rest of its properties are, we can only faintly guess. We have only one key. In ourselves we can observe both the inner reality of a thing and its external and visible symbol. A delicate galvanometer may show the current impulse travelling along a nerve which we perceive as a spasm of pain. The pain is a reality, the current is the symbol of that reality, which may thus become evident to senses other than our own. But the sensations involved in reading a galvanometer are quite different from the sensation of pain. Both sensations are realities, but of quite a different kind. So different may be the reality underlying any "material" phenomenon from the effects presented to our senses.

Dr. Johnstone Stoney,[1] who has, perhaps, done more than any living physicist to elucidate the connection between mental realities (" auta ") and the physical universe, puts the matter as follows :—

"The only part of the stupendous autic universe (universe of realities) which a human being can *adequately* examine is that excessively small group of auta which are the thoughts of his own mind, with the similarly small groups that are the minds of his fellow man and of some other animals; he cannot even make any adequate study of the events that go on within the synergos [subconscious self] which is so closely associated with his mind, and can only collect mere scraps of information as to what the real events are throughout the rest of the vast machine. As to that tiny group of auta that are one human being's thoughts, it bears

---

[1] *Proceedings of the American Philosophical Society*, April 3, 1903.

somewhat the same relation to the mighty whole of the autic universe as . . . some of the more slowly changing events within the cortex of the brain bears to the enormous totality of motions that are going on objectively throughout the whole of nature. This makes it evident that the part of the autic universe that man can adequately examine is but one drop of an immeasurable ocean, and although that little drop is an actual specimen of the kind of things that auta are, it is very plain that we are not justified in assuming that it is a fair average specimen of them."

The only path open to us if we want to get at the reality underlying physical appearances is to carefully note our own thoughts and their physical accompaniments. Once we know the mental phenomena which accompany any given physical process in our brain, we may hope to interpret other physical phenomena in terms of mental realities, and thus arrive at their real significance.

"Working under these disadvantages," proceeds Dr. Stoney, "man (and the same is true of the more intelligent of the lower animals) has constructed the Physical Hypothesis whereby to enable him to form a correct forecast of the changes which will occur in nature. The physical hypothesis is the supposition *that the objects of nature can act on one another,* either directly (action at a distance) or through intervening media (which by many is supposed to be an essentially different kind of action). Now the objects of nature are syntheta of perceptions and ultra - perceptions ; and syntheta of perceptions cannot be what really act. Nevertheless, it is eminently useful to carry on our investigation under the physical hypothesis that it is they which act, and to confine our efforts to tracing out what effects this action must be supposed capable of producing, and under what laws it must operate, in order that it may account for what occurs in nature."

This distinction should be carefully borne in mind when we approach *ultimate* natural processes. There has been a great deal of superficial and dogmatic utterance concerning ultimate realities. We need only cite the declaration that action at a distance is impossible and unthinkable, or that consciousness and mental action generally *consist* of motions of particles, which is much like saying that a wind consists of weathercocks. A human crowd may, for police purposes, often be regarded as a viscous stream of particles of uniform size, subjected to a certain pressure, and obeying certain laws of flow. But that does not exhaust the whole nature of a crowd. In the same way, our physical theories may work with inert atoms and electrons without troubling about the ultimate reality at the back of them. If there is such a reality behind them, it will, to judge from all natural analogy, be something in the nature of thought or will. A jug, a road, a house, a lathe are embodiments of some human will. Why should not other objects, equally "substantial," be the embodiments of some will different from our own? Our next step in the exploration of the universe must be to get at its inner soul and meaning. So far we have only examined, so to speak, its size and shape, its clothing, its gait. We must now get to a bowing acquaintance, and by-and-by we must get into conversation.

The exploration of the infra-world has given us a vivid realisation of the relativity of time and space, and has, I maintain, definitely delivered us from the apparent necessity of providing a given time for a given spell of existence. Life is thus to a great extent delivered from the trammels of time, while at the same time absolved from the confinement of space. Life is superior both to space and time. This has been instinctively felt by advanced minds in all ages; but here, perhaps, we have for the first time a physical justification for such belief.

It will, perhaps, be useful here to resume the main conclusions of this essay :—

(1) The visible universe is only one in a chain of similar universes contained one within the other, and differing only in the size of their elementary constituent particles.

(2) The atoms of one universe are the suns of the next finer universe; the electrons are its planets.

(3) The unit of time is reduced in the same proportion as the unit of length, leaving the velocities as usual.

(4) Space and time are relative, but velocity is absolute.

(5) The next universe below ours in the scale of sizes may be called the infra-world.

II

THE SUPRA-WORLD

CHAPTER I

BEYOND THE STARS

In the preceding description of the infra-world I followed a line of reasoning which led to the conclusion that by descending in order of magnitude far below the smallest microscopic object until we reach the world of atoms, we discover a world which in all probability, is not essentially different from the world we live in, and may possibly be almost identical in most of its astronomical, physical, and chemical conditions with our own visible universe. I endeavoured, by reasoning from the known laws of electricity and chemistry, to ascertain the forces at play in that "infra-world." The most curious and important result so obtained was that events happen as much faster in the infra-world as the sizes are smaller. The ratio for both is $10^{22}:1$. Since the velocities of atoms turn out to be of the same order as our "planetary" velocities (about 20 miles per second), there was good reason to assume that all velocities remain about the same, and since the resistance of the ether to velocities greater than 186,000 miles per second is infinite, it was natural to assume that in both worlds there is the same limit of speed, and hence also the same ether.

I now propose to proceed in the opposite direction along the scale of magnitude, and to investigate the conditions met with when, instead of dividing all sizes by 10,000 trillion, we enlarge them in that proportion. I shall endeavour to show that we then arrive at another world comparable with our own, which I propose to call the supra-world.

A dried currant has a roughly elliptical shape, its dimensions varying from 0·3 cm. to 1 cm. Now enlarge this by the " world-ratio " 10^{22}. It will then become a body filling up the whole visible universe out to the uttermost star visible in the most powerful telescope, or recorded by the longest photographic exposure. Its 20,000 trillion atoms, if shining with " infra-light," will, seen from within, become a splendid starry vault, emitting the blaze of a bright noonday, the stars being much more densely crowded than those of the Milky Way.

What changes will this starry world undergo in a second of time? Obviously, the revolutions of the stars which were once atoms will be much slower than heretofore, and, however fast the motions of the atoms or stars may be, they will be less effective in producing a given change of configuration in the proportion familiar to us from the infra-world— viz., 10^{22}. Whatever changes a currant undergoes in a second of our time will now be spread over a period of 10^{22} seconds, or a thousand billion years. Now the currant evinces no perceptible change to us in one second, and if our starry heavens did actually constitute some piece of organic matter such as a currant, we need not expect any very marked changes in it for a period of time far exceeding the longest geological epoch ever postulated.

To complete the analogy between a small material body like a lentil or a currant and the visible universe, one essential element is wanting. The density of a currant is slightly greater than that of water. The density of the whole visible universe is much less than that. We have already seen that in descending to the infra-world the densities increase 10^{11} times. In ascending to the supra-world they decrease in at least the same proportion. If they did not do so, the velocities would not remain of the same order as those we are familiar with, but would all tend to approach the velocity of light.

Now let us go through the converse process, and reduce the visible universe by the world-ratio, or, what comes to the same thing, increase our own size in the same ratio, taking care to alter the scale of time correspondingly. What should we find ?

We should find a small ring, much too small to go on our finger, but showing very intricate and what some people might be disposed to call "artistic"

workmanship, floating in space, or falling through it.
We cannot even remotely guess what is becoming of
the ring, since its fate for a single supra-second takes
a thousand billion of our years to evolve itself. But
we can see it on every starlight night. The ring is
known as the Milky Way. Its density is much
greater than that of the rest of the starry heavens.
Indeed, it probably is the only object we should
perceive at all, the rest of the stars being as
negligible as the air contained within a ring lying
on a table.

What else should we see? What would the rest
of the supra-world be like?

According to Newcomb and Wallace, there is
nothing else to see, or, if there is, it is quite invisible
from our earth. It seems presumptuous for any
mere mortal to assert that our universe is limited
by the ring of the Milky Way, but the argument
is convincing enough. Miss A. M. Clerke, in her
"Systems of the Stars," puts it as follows: "The
sidereal world presents us, to all appearance, with
a finite system. . . . The probability amounts almost
to certainty that star-strewn space is of measurable
dimensions. For from innumerable stars a limitless
sum total of radiation should be derived, by which
darkness would be banished from our skies; and the
'intense inane,' glowing with the mingled beams of
suns individually indistinguishable, would bewilder
our feeble senses with its monotonous splendour. . . .

Unless, that is to say, light suffers some degree of enfeeblement in space. . . . But there is not a particle of evidence that any such toll is exacted; contrary indications are strong; and the assertion that its payment is inevitable depends upon analogies which may be wholly visionary. We are then, for the present, entitled to disregard the problematical effect of a more than dubious cause."

Wallace[1] advances three other arguments in support of the finality of our stellar universe:—

"(1) In various parts of the heavens there are areas of considerable extent, besides rifts, lanes, or circular patches, where stars are either quite absent or very faint and few in number. We look, in fact, through these 'holes in the heavens' into the starless depths of space beyond.

"(2) There is a steady increase in the number of stars down to the ninth or tenth magnitudes. Then it suddenly changes, and the number of stars of magnitudes down to the seventeenth is only about one-tenth of what it would have been had the same ratio of increase continued. The conclusion is that the fainter stars are more thinly scattered in space.

"(3) The total amount of light given by all stars of a given magnitude is twice as much as that of all stars two magnitudes higher in the scale. If

[1] Sir A. R. Wallace, F.R.S., " Man's Place in the Universe."

this increase were maintained down to the seventeenth magnitude, the light of all stars combined should be seven times as great as moonlight, whereas, in reality, it is only one-twentieth."

All these arguments are, of course, purely optical. They fall to the ground as soon as we admit the possibility of further stellar universes consisting of dark stars. Our own stellar system contains vast numbers of such bodies, and there is no reason why a stellar system should not be free from light of that particular wave-length which impresses our eyes or our photographic plates. For aught we know, the luminosity of our stellar system may be a very temporary affair. Lord Kelvin estimates the life of our sun as 50 to 100 million years a period which, on the supra-world scale, would amount to about a ten-millionth of a second.

There is, of course another possibility. If the world was created 100,000 years ago, then no light from bodies nore than 100,000 light-years away from us could possibly have reached us up to the present; but light from stars further and further away would be continually arriving at the earth's surface, and thus our vision into space, confined at present by the Milky Way, would be expanding at the rate of 186,000 miles per second. That possibility would become a probability if at any time a great cluster of stars were to become visible, and remain visible, without showing any evidence of collision, like the ordinary " new star."

The root-hypothesis of this work is, however, that this world of ours is a good average sample of the universe, as it always has existed, and always will continue to exist, and that, however high we ascend, or however low we descend, in the scale of magnitude, we may hope to find conditions not alarmingly different from those which we have here and now learnt to know and to adapt ourselves to. I am disposed to believe that this place in which I am, and this moment in which I write, are as significant, as sacred, and as important as any I have ever had, or am ever likely to get. There may be variety, improvement, progress, or decay, but the essential elements of all these I believe to be permanent, and not confined to the Here and Now.

Let us not be afraid of extending the scope of scientific inquiry, and of applying known laws to wider ranges until new limits confront us. Newton made the law of gravitation include the solar system. Spectroscopy has applied our terrestrial chemistry to the sun and stars. Meteorites bring us samples of interplanetary matter, and we find nothing but materials well known on earth. Why should mere magnitude appal us ? Size is only relative. The Arabic numerals and the exponential notation enable us to state the largest magnitudes in simpler terms than those of an ordinary balance-sheet. Why should we draw the line before Nature draws it for us?

For an average span of some thirty to fifty years we are landed on this particular planet, and provided with the necessary organs to carry on a certain average set of activities. When we are withdrawn from this world we may have other senses, organs, and activities. The change will be great and far-reaching, and may, for aught we know, cut off all communication between us and the visible universe. We may be landed in some other link of the chain of worlds, or in an entirely different kind of world. That reflection should prevent our having any hesitation to postulate the unity and sameness of the universe accessible to our present set of senses. There is quite enough liberty in store for us without looking to the distant stars and the high heavens for it. In assuming, therefore, the essential sameness of the visible universe throughout all possible magnitudes, and, as a corollary, its eternity and infinite stability, we are not renouncing all higher states of existence, nor confining our future life to an endless repetition of accustomed detail and drudgery. All we postulate is that the present world is uniform in space and time. Of all possible worlds in which we might (and may yet) be placed, it is for us here and now the most worthy of investigation. Our sense of unity demands that it should have an absolute and permanent value in the total system of the universe, and this will be greatly enhanced if it can be shown that its laws are not subject to revision, and that the universal writ runs to the furthest boundaries which the imagination can conceive.

CHAPTER II

In 1786 William Herschel remarked that he had discovered fifteen hundred universes. He referred, of course, to as many nebulæ, which he believed to be galaxies external to our own. But, in any case, it is risky to use the word universe in the plural number without some special definition. If by "universe" we mean the totality of things, there can, of course, be only one totality. But if we mean by "universe" the sum total of things accessible to our senses, or, in other words, the aggregate of those things of which we can now or at any time have cognisance, then that very human "universe" may be imagined to exist side by side or interwoven with other universes, accessible to different sets of senses, whether of beings lower or higher than ourselves. In that sense, the infra-world is a distinct universe interpenetrating our own, just as our human or "visible" universe, the world we live in, interpenetrates the supra-world. As already pointed out, our faculties are in touch with the confines of both the other worlds. The smallest perceptible length and the greatest measurable distance measure corresponding quantities. The smallest cluster of atoms visible and measurable in the microscope is at one end of the scale, and our stellar system, itself a cluster of stellar "atoms," is at the other. But if we want to extend our investigations into the supra-world itself we must transcend the stellar system, just as, in our exploration of the infra-world, we had to descend far below the smallest microscopic object. Our guides into the unknown were the known laws of electricity and chemistry, which enabled us to draw conclusions concerning objects individually concealed from our senses. These same physical laws shall be our guides into the supra-world.

In dealing with ultra-stellar distances, I do not propose to interlard my remarks with wondering contemplations of the awfulness of spatial vastnesses. It is not because I am less reverent than other people, but because I find other objects of reverence than mere size. To worship mere size is a relic of barbarism. There is nothing inherently appalling in the infinite or the infinitesimal. Size is purely relative. We must resolutely refuse to be overwhelmed by figures. To me a figure ceases to be overwhelming as soon as it is expressible in concise notation, exponential or otherwise. And even infinity itself is a mathematical quantity which algebra has deprived of most of its terrors.

We start with the assumption that our stellar

system, limited by the Milky Way, is a very small portion of the next higher universe, the "supra-world." Our first task is then to inquire what is outside it.

It has been shown with mathematical certainty that if infinite space were strewn with stars, as is our stellar system, and if these stars shone like our stars, and if they had existed for all eternity, then the appearance of the sky would be one blaze of sunlight throughout. To this I may add the equally certain conclusion that every part of space, including the earth and ourselves, would be at a white heat and gaseous; for radiant heat would be propagated in the same way as light. And, further, that the circumstance of space being cold can be used as a conclusive proof of the absence of any sensible loss of radiation through absorption in space; for the absorbing medium would be heated by the process of absorption, and would then itself radiate the heat inwards upon our devoted heads. The only things that could effectually shield us from the intolerable blaze of infinity would be either (1) a gap in the ether all round our stellar system, or (2) a perfectly reflecting surface surrounding it, a kind of Ptolemaic "firmament" in a new sense, and for a novel purpose.

Both of these contrivances would work both ways, and would preserve the light and heat of our own stellar system from dissipation. But this at once suggests a fairly conclusive argument against either possibility. Whenever energy is radiated by wave-motion, and the waves arrive at the limit of the medium capable of transmitting the motion, they are totally reflected. And whether we have an etherless envelope round our system or a perfect reflector, we must expect to receive from it a uniform faint luminosity and a uniform slight heat. Whatever may be said about the real source of the so-called stellar heat, there is no doubt that the faint luminosity is entirely wanting in many parts of the heavens. Vega gives us about the same quantity of heat as a candle ten miles away, and Arcturus double that quantity. In the starless portions of the sky no radiant heat is discoverable. If it exists, it is below the limits of our measuring instruments. This suggests, therefore, that if there is a supra-world, it is a cold and dark world, or, at least, that it would appear cold and dark to us. Not so, as we shall see, to its own inhabitants.

Our measuring instruments of light and heat fail, so far, to establish the existence of anything outside our stellar system. On the other hand, they do not disprove the existence of a whole surrounding universe of stellar systems which are comparatively dark and cold. But our theoretical resources are not yet exhausted. Wherever we have a force or form of energy whose action across interstellar space is known, we may employ that agency for testing

the existence of remote worlds. Besides radiation,
we have gravitation, electrostatic force, electro-
dynamic ("magnetic") force, and magnetic induc-
tion. All these may yet be used to explore the
supra-world; but in these infantile days of cosmic
electricity, we must perforce be content with reasoning based upon Newton's law of gravitation.

Lord Kelvin[1] has made an interesting essay in
this direction. Assuming the farthest star to have
a parallax of 0·001 of a second, which would imply
a distance of 3×10^{21} cm., and that a sphere of that
radius surrounding our stellar system contains 100
million stars of about the same average mass as
the sun, he shows that the mean force of gravitational attraction over the surface of that sphere
is $1 \cdot 37 \times 10^{-11}$ times that of gravity at the earth's
surface. It follows that a body falling into this
sphere from infinite outer space would have a
speed of some 11 km. (seven miles) per second
—just about double the planetary velocity of
Neptune.

Meteoric speeds go up to 40 km. per second;
but their speed is acquired under the attraction
and in the proximity of the sun. The solar system
is, according to Campbell, moving with a velocity
of 19·89 km. per second towards a point in R.A.
277° 30′ and Dec. 19° 58′ N. The proper motions
of stars show an average velocity of 21 miles per

[1] *Philosophical Magazine*, August 1901.

second, though 1830 Groombridge is credited with the extraordinary speed of 59 miles per second, and the spectroscopic binary Lacaille 3105 with a relative velocity of 380 miles a second. All these speeds fall far short of the speed of light, which we now believe to be the unattainable limit of speed of all material things.

An important conclusion may be drawn at once from the observation that no stellar velocities exceed $\frac{1}{300}$th of the velocity of light. It is that *the mass comprised within a world-sphere increases as its radius, and not as its volume,* or in other words, that *the density within a world-sphere varies inversely as the surface of the sphere.* By " world-sphere " I mean a sphere enclosing a " visible universe " of any order.

To make this clearer, we will assume that space is strewn with other stellar systems comparable to our own, and that some 100 million of these systems make up a galaxy of their own. Instead of a sphere of 3×10^{21} cm., we might have a sphere 3×10^{31} cm. in radius. We can hardly assume this sphere to have the same average density as our own stellar system, since all appearances are against it. If it had, however, we should have a mass 10^{30} times as large as before, and the energy of a body falling to its surface from infinity would be 10^{30} times what it is at the limit of our stellar system. Its theoretical speed would be 10^{10} times

seven miles per second.   This speed, of course, it
could never attain, nor a 100,000th part of it, on
account of the resistance of the ether; but it would
have a speed very closely approaching that of light,
and the vast majority of bodies in our stellar
system would be found to possess some such
velocity.   If, on the other hand, the density varied
inversely as the surface, and the mass embraced
simply as the radius, then the gravitational potential at the surface would be always the same, being
proportional to the mass and inversely proportional
to the distance.   And, as a consequence, stellar
velocities approaching the velocity of light would
not prevail in any part of the universe.

   Now, the actual average density of the stellar
system by the above figures is 3×10^{-22}, as com-
pared with water.   But we know that the mass
of the stellar system is largely concentrated in the
Milky Way, and the density of the latter is probably
not much smaller than a billionth of that of water.
And since the Milky Way must be taken as repre-
senting one of the "objects" of the supra-world,
it is interesting to note that its density is less than
terrestrial densities in about the same proportion
as the densities of the "infra-world" are greater.

CHAPTER III

BEFORE endeavouring to interpret the structure and history of our present stellar system, it will be necessary to dispose of certain questions with regard to its limits, which have been much debated of late. Alfred R. Wallace has dealt very fully with the question of the unity or plurality of worlds in his well-known work on "Man's Place in the Universe." With the balance of probabilities in favour of organic life in other planets than ours we are here not concerned. Our scale of life—life in the supra-world—will transcend a quadrillionfold the scale of human life. But before we can describe life in the supra-world in terms more or less borrowed from our own, we must make sure that our supra-world exists—or, at the least, that its existence is not out of harmony with known laws of nature.

But what are these laws? There's the rub. For when it comes to travelling beyond the confines of the galaxy, travelling a billion times as far as its outer edge, in order to arrive at last on the surface of a "supra-star," we cannot pin our faith exclusively to any one of the great world-laws so far dis-

covered.   Transmission of light?   Who knows but
that the interstellar luminiferous ether may thin out
and finally forsake us !   The law of gravitation ?
Men like Wallace and Whittaker are willing to
abandon it before they have got as far as the
galaxy !   Yet it seems as if these two agencies must
be our chief, perhaps our only, guides in exploring
ultra-galactic space.   We must, therefore, deal with
them at some further length.

   Transmission of Light.—One of the most powerful
arguments against the existence of ultra-galactic
universes is based upon the laws of the transmission
of light.   This argument, already referred to, dis-
proves the existence of luminous stars throughout
infinite space, by pointing out that the sky would
then have a uniform brightness equal to that of the
sun in every part.   The value of this argument
depends upon the truth of the following assumptions :—

   1. That the luminiferous ether pervades all space.
   2. That the number of dark bodies is comparatively small.
   3. That the stars are irregularly distributed.
   4. That luminous stars have an eternal existence.
   The first assumption certainly appeals to our imagination, and no valid argument has been brought
up against it.   The third assumption is sometimes
overlooked.   It is obvious that an infinite line of
stars might exist behind every star in the heavens

without our becoming aware of it. But the extreme improbability of such an arrangement may encourage us to take the irregularity of distribution for granted. The fourth assumption is one that does not commend itself to any one who looks for a definite epoch at which the visible universe was created. But to any one familiar with the line of reasoning derived from atomic conditions, the eternity of stars must appear extremely probable, whatever may be said of their luminosity or their individual fate.

The second assumption is, I think, the most important, as it bears upon the validity of the law of gravitation.

Suppose that the number of dark stars in the Milky Way exceeded the bright ones by 1000 : 1, and that there was a greater preponderance elsewhere, sufficient to bring the density of our stellar system up to about 10^{-11}, water being unity. In other words, out of every 100,000 million cubic miles of stellar space, one cubic mile would be occupied by the material of a star, a planet, or a dark sun of the average density of water. The assumption contains nothing very improbable: the number of dark bodies is suspected to be very large in any case, and even a gréat preponderance would not materially increase the occultations and variabilities usually observed.

Now it is obvious that if all space were uniformly strewn with bright stars, many of these would at any given moment be obscured by dark ones. If we assume that the dark stars have the same average sectional area as the sun, it is easy to calculate how far we can see into space before our vision is completely obscured by the dark bodies. The distance comes out, according to the distribution of the dark bodies, as between 100 and 10,000 light-years, or just about the distance of the inner and outer edges of the galaxy.[1]

This system would account completely for the apparent limitation of the universe. The fact of many of the brightest stars, like Canopus, being so far away as to have no appreciable parallax would be accounted for by the accident of their light not being intercepted by dark bodies. The laws of distribution of light by magnitudes would be explained, or, at least, not contradicted. "Rifts" and "holes in the heavens" would be interpreted as accumulations of dark bodies, and the most powerful telescopes, instead of piercing through the star-veil into empty space, would penetrate so far as the black wall which cuts us off from the ultra-galactic worlds.

But how will this system fare against the arguments of infinity ? The optical argument advanced by Newcomb no longer affects it, since the light from outer galaxies is completely intercepted. But the thermal objection might still hold good, and

[1] See Note A at end of this chapter.

does hold good against an infinite universe of hot stars, which would keep us at a white heat, in spite of our protecting wall. But if a hot star is something altogether exceptional—a freak happening once in a billion times—then the average temperature of an infinite universe will be quite comfortable, and, indeed, extremely stable and permanent.

The laws of radiation, therefore, furnish no argument against the existence of an infinite series of galaxies outside our own, so long as we regard the dark star as the prevailing type. But the case may be further investigated by means of the argument from gravitation.

The Law of Gravitation.—Newton's law of gravitation asserts that every heavenly body attracts every other heavenly body with a force proportional to the product of their masses, and inversely proportional to the square of their distance apart. This law has, so far, been confirmed for distances ranging from 1 cm. to about 10^{19} cm.—truly a vast range. At distances less than 1 cm. it appears to be replaced, or, at least, complicated, by the very much more powerful electric forces brought into play, and, as regards distances beyond ten light-years, we have as yet no evidence of its validity. At distances of the order of 10^{-22} cm., a force 10^{33} times more powerful takes the place of gravitation, and rules the orbits of the infra-world. What happens at distances of 10^{22} cm. and beyond?

Can it be that gravitation becomes 10^{33} times feebler than it is in more accessible places? Upon an answer to this question depends any real progress we may make in our demonstration of a supra-world. At present we can only indicate two or three alternative probabilities, one or the other of which is more probable than the rest.

The argument from gravitation is so ingenious and comparatively new, that it will, perhaps, be useful to state it in full and in simple language.

Let there be only two bodies in space, one about the size of the sun, and having a mass of 10^{33} grammes, and the other a mass of 1 gramme, situated at a practically infinite distance, so far away that the attraction between them is immeasurably small. Now let the gramme fall towards the sun. Its velocity, at first excessively slow, will gradually increase, and its acceleration will also increase as it approaches the sun and the force between them increases. To calculate the actual speed of the gramme at any given distance from the sun may appear a task of formidable difficulty, and requiring high mathematical training. But it is made really very simple by the theory of potential, which plays such an important and useful part in the science of electricity.[1]

Take the limit of 10,000 light-years or 10^{22} cm., and suppose, with Lord Kelvin, that a sphere of

[1] See Note B at end of this chapter.

this radius contains no masses but the visible stars, about 100 million in number, and possessing an aggregate mass of 10^{42} grammes. A strange body falling from infinite space into the outskirts of this system will acquire a velocity of

$$\sqrt{\frac{2 \times 6 \cdot 66 \times 10^{-8} \times 10^{42}}{10^{22}}}$$

centimetres per second, or $36 \cdot 5 \times 10^5$ cm. per second, or $36 \cdot 5$ km. or $22\frac{1}{2}$ miles per second—about the speed of the earth, and quite a reasonable and usual speed. If space is universally filled with stars to the same extent as our stellar system, there will be no free fall from infinite space, and no speed to be got from the attraction of our particular galaxy. Yet speeds of the same order will be generated under the force of attraction of the various suns, and nothing will be altered by adding galaxies upon galaxies, so long as it is done consistently and uniformly throughout infinite space. But supposing that we stop at a distance of 10^{26} cm., increasing the radius 10,000 times, then we increase the mass a billion times, the potential at the limit 100 million times, and the resulting speed 10,000 times. Thus the speed will be 225,000 miles per second. This speed is some 40,000 miles per second above that of light, and therefore, by all accounts, quite impossible. The result will be that all foreign bodies will enter our system with a velocity closely approaching that of light, and even within the system such velocities must be very prevalent. That this is not the case tells heavily against the possibility of a stellar aggregation isolated in space, and much larger than the visible universe.

The same argument is strengthened a million-fold when we deal with a galactic system of the density 10^{-11} instead of 10^{-22}. This would give a mass of 10^{53} grammes to our galactic system, and a velocity of over seven million miles per second, and very much more in a larger system of equal density.

These considerations effectively dispose of our dark and comparatively dense supra-world, unless that world is uniform and unlimited throughout space. But as regards uniformity, one look at the starry heavens will banish all hope of it. If anything is certain, it is the infinite variety of the universe. If uniformity had existed at any time, the chances are overwhelming in favour of its having rapidly disappeared. And this brings us to a third line of argument.

Stability.—Those philosophers who start from "creation," and date it a few hundred million years ago—a mere flash in the stellar scale of time—have the great advantage of starting from some point of uniformity, and ending in a final cataclysm. But the purpose of these chapters is to transcend, as far as possible, the barriers of space and time, to emphasise their relativity, and to increase our outlook to several orders of infinity. Whatever system we ultimately adopt as our theory of the universe must, therefore, not only be in accord with present-day laws and agencies, but must be the logical outcome of those same agencies working for all eternity.

On this point, Alfred R. Wallace, in his great work referred to above, says :—

"One of the greatest difficulties with regard to the vast system of stars around us is the question of its permanence and stability, if not absolutely and indefinitely, yet for periods sufficiently long to allow for the many millions of years that have certainly been required for our terrestrial life-development. This period, in the case of the earth, as I have sufficiently shown, has been characterised throughout by extreme uniformity, while a continuance of that uniformity for a few million years in the future is almost equally certain.

But our mathematical astronomers can find no indications of such stability of the stellar universe as a whole, if subject to the law of gravitation alone. In reply to some questions on this point, my friend, Professor George Darwin, writes as follows : "A symmetrical annular system of bodies might revolve in a circle with or without a central body. Such a system would be unstable. If the bodies are of unequal masses and not symmetrically dis-

H

posed, the break-up of the system would probably
be more rapid than in the ideal case of sym-
metry. . . ."

This would imply that the great annular system
of the Milky Way is unstable.   But if so, its existence at all is a greater mystery than ever. . . .
Mr. E. T. Whittaker (secretary to the Royal
Astronomical Society), to whom Professor G.
Darwin sent my questions, writes : " I doubt
whether the principal phenomena of the stellar
universe are consequences of the law of gravitation at all. . . . In fact, it may be questioned
whether, for bodies of such tremendous extent
as the Milky Way or Nebulæ, the effect which we
call gravitation is given by Newton's law; just
as the ordinary formulæ of electrostatic attraction
break down when we consider charges moving
with very great velocities."

In spite of these doubts, it behoves us to cling
as long as possible to Newton's great generalisation, and only to abandon it when by doing so we
attain a greater.

When, instead of a few million years, we draw
upon all eternity for our resources in time, we
actually meet with some simplifications rather
than the reverse.   The first of these is that the
present moment does not differ from any previous
moment in the universe as a whole.   Whatever
has been, is, and will be.   Our galactic system

cannot be the only system of luminous stars in the infinite universe ever evolved. That would distinguish our present epoch above any other. Special cases must oscillate about the average, both in space and time. There is no *unique* epoch in the universe. If there were, the whole system would be unstable, and subject to sudden and overwhelming changes. The constancy of the laws governing the infra - world through vast stretches of atomic time is a lesson for us, teaching to look for no catastrophes or specially-favoured times in our own world.

This consideration is fatal to the "single-world" theory. The galactic system is unstable. It cannot last. It must change into something entirely different—perhaps, according to some, into a single sun 1000 times as large as our sun, radiating off its heat into empty space, and hanging, at the end of a billion years, alone in a vast void, itself a gigantic kind of moon, scarred and crumbling, the last inhabitant, rayless and forlorn, of a dark and empty nothingness.

If this can happen, why should it happen just then? Why did it not happen a billion years ago? Because it was not then created? And why not? Why should this vast universe, with its millionfold life, be crowded into one short moment —a moment of infinitesimal duration for any one gifted with time-perception on the stellar scale?

It is unthinkable. The mind stands more aghast at such a possibility than it does at the contemplation of many infinities. No; there must be a supra-world—a world of a higher scale, inhabited by beings for whom a trillion years are as a day, and the sun's life-period the shortest measurable interval of time. Already there are at least two schemes of such a world in sight. It remains for us to choose the most plausible one, and, if possible, the reality.

NOTE A.

Since the "dark-star" argument has been the centre of considerable controversy, I may as well give the figures here.

Ten thousand light-years are approximately 10^{22} cm. A sphere of that radius contains $4 \cdot 2 \times 10^{66}$ cubic cm. The density being 10^{-11}, the mass contained within this sphere is $4 \cdot 2 \times 10^{35}$ grammes. This is about 10^{22} times the mass of our sun, so that if the sun represents a fair average, there will be 10^{22} heavenly bodies within that sphere—a number very largely in excess of the luminous stars. Now, the sectional area of the sun is 6×10^{22} sq. cm., and the sectional area of all the 10^{22} bodies added up is 6×10^{44} sq. cm. The surface of a sphere of 10^{22} cm. radius is $12 \cdot 6 \times 10^{44}$ sq. cm. So that if all the dark bodies were evenly distributed over this surface, they would cover half of it. But that would be their least effective position, and many of them, being nearer to us, would cover more of the heavenly vault. A body brought within 5000 light-years would be four times as effective as before. So we may safely say that, given a distribution of stars as supposed, both luminous and dark, *our vision would be absolutely blocked at the actual limit of the galaxy.*

NOTE B.

The energy possessed by a body of m grammes flying with a velocity of v cm. per second is equal to $\frac{1}{2}mv^2$ ergs. If we, therefore, measure the velocity of the gramme falling towards the sun at any particular instant, we know its energy of motion—in other words, the amount of energy it has acquired under the sun's attraction since it started from infinite space. The amount of this energy is, of course, quite definite and measurable for any point in space, and is called the "gravitational potential" due to the sun at that point. The gravitational potential due to a body at any point is inversely proportional to the distance of that point.[1] In figures, it is expressed by $\frac{GM}{D}$, where M is the mass of the attracting body, D the distance of the point in space, and G the "gravitational constant" which fixes the numerical value of the potential for the particular units adopted. When the mass is expressed in grammes, and the distance in centimetres, G is $6 \cdot 66 \times 10^{-8}$. Thus, at the distance of

[1] An elementary proof of this useful theorem is given in Chapter III. of my " Electron Theory," p. 45.

10^{13} cm. (about the distance of the earth from the sun) the potential is—

$$\frac{6.66 \times 10^{-8} \times 10^{33}}{10^{13}} = 6.66 \times 10^{12}.$$

The work done by the sun in accelerating any body from infinity may thus be measured by multiplying this number by the mass of the body in grammes. And this work will be embodied in the energy of motion thus acquired. For a mass of m grammes we have therefore—

$$\tfrac{1}{2}mv^2 = m \times 6.66 \times 10^{12}$$
or—
$$v^2 = 2 \times 6.66 \times 10^{12}$$

Extracting the square root on both sides, we get $v = 3.64 \times 10^6$, or 36.4 km. per second, or $22\tfrac{1}{2}$ miles per second. This, as might have been expected, is not far from the earth's speed in its orbit. For the speed may be that of motion in any direction, so long as it is the same for a given distance from the sun. To put the whole relation into one formula, we have—

$$v = \sqrt{\frac{2\mathrm{GM}}{\mathrm{D}}}$$

from which we may at once derive a few important rules :—

1. The speed at any given distance is proportional to the square root of the central mass.

2. It is proportional to the square root of the gravitational constant.

3. It is inversely proportional to the square root of the distance. The actual force of attraction between two masses M and m at distance D is equal to $\frac{\mathrm{GM}m}{\mathrm{D}^2}$. The force is in dynes, the masses in

grammes, and the distance in centimetres. To convert to pounds and inches, G must be made 0.47×10^{-8}.

Here, then, we have a basis for extending our gravitational arguments into the uttermost vastnesses of space.

CHAPTER IV

SUPRA-STARS AND LIVING GALAXIES

WE have now to proceed in making our final choice between the various solutions presented by the problem of the Infinite Universe. We shall assume:—

1. That the material universe is infinite in three-dimensional space, and eternal both in the past and the future.

2. That the law of gravitation holds good throughout infinite time and space.

3. That the luminiferous ether has the same properties throughout space.

These assumptions have already been shown to be well founded. Gravitation and the propagation of light are the same for all parts of the stellar system hitherto explored, and even in spectroscopic binaries we have enough material to show that their orbits are conic sections. We know that the only laws of central force under which a body will have such an orbit for all initial conditions are: (1) Newton's law of gravitation, and (2) the law according to which the force is *directly pro-*

portional to the distance, and this latter alternative is sufficiently excluded.

The infinity and eternity of the universe implies the absence of special "points of singularity," such as general catastrophes or absolute uniformity. Whatever variety exists in space and time is equalised if we take the space large enough or the time long enough. The world of the present moment is instinct with life and energy, with change and progress and decay, bewildering and overwhelming to the finite mind. But the infinite universe is unchanging. It is the same yesterday, to-day, and for ever. There is no loss and no gain; there is only redistribution and circulation. There is a fundamental and abiding constancy, and yet the variety is infinite. The All is immutable, but the detail is for ever new. The equilibrium is eternal; but the event, the incident, the individuality is unique, unprecedented, irrecoverable.

I have proved that there are two solutions which are in accordance with the above assumptions. The first of these postulates a comparatively dense universe of a consistency somewhat greater than that of the Milky Way, but containing dark stars in large excess. The other (p. 103) implies that in proceeding out into space the matter included in successive world-spheres must vary, not as the volume but as the radius; in other words, that in the universes of successively higher orders the densities must be less. In the absence of evidence for a vast preponderance of dark stars within our own galactic system, I prefer to adopt this latter alternative. It gives scope for greater variety, it is more probable from the point of view of stability, and it is in harmony with that general prevalence of *separate objects* which we discern throughout nature, whether in atoms, living beings, stars, or galaxies.

We have throughout this work equated stars (or rather solar systems) with chemical atoms, an identification which is well supported by electrical and chemical data. The average diameter of an atom is 10^{-8} cm. The diameter of the solar system is about 10^{14} cm. The ratio of these two quantities is 10^{22}. This is the "world ratio" which I have hitherto applied to all phenomena in successive universes. Using this as a guide, it is not very difficult to construct our "supra-world."

There is our galactic system, our "visible universe," measuring 10^{21} or 10^{22} cm. across, a distance corresponding on our human scale to 1 mm. or 1 cm., or, say, $\frac{1}{8}$ in. To a "supra-man," therefore, our galaxy will be a small object of about that size. It contains about 1000 million stars, or about as many stars as the lowliest organism known to us contains atoms. For aught we know it may *be* an organism—a fascinating question with which I shall deal further on.

Outside the galaxy is empty space for some distance, and then other galaxies or somewhat different structures. These again must form a larger aggregate, something we might call a "supra-star." The diameters of the heavenly bodies known to us average about 10^{10} cm. Hence, by the "world-ratio," we must expect the diameter of the supra-star to be somewhere about 10^{32} cm., or a hundred billion light-years.

The mass of our galactic system is nearly 10^{42} grammes. By our argument from the law of gravitation, the mass within the supra-star must be as much greater as its diameter is greater. This makes the mass of the supra-star 10^{58} grammes and its density 10^{-44}. The velocity acquired by a body in falling from infinity to the surface of the supra-star would be some 60 miles per second, and might rise to 120 miles in penetrating to its interior. This is not excessive in comparison with observed "proper motions."

The mass of the supra-star being 10^{58} grammes, it contains 10^{11} times the mass of our galaxy. We might say it contains 100,000 million galaxies. The density of the galaxy being 10^{22} times that of the supra-star, each galaxy will have 10^{22} times its own volume to move about in without collision. The average distance of the nearest galaxy will be about ten million times the diameter of our galaxy, or, say 10,000 million light-years, so that, if the nearest galaxy happened to have consisted of luminous stars for several thousand million years, but no longer, it would still be quite invisible to us. And when we consider that it would, in all probability, take a billion years for two galaxies to approach each other and meet, we can understand that such an event must be a rare occurrence. Rare as it is, Prof. Kapteyn and Mr. Eddington have found some evidence to show that it is taking place in our own system.

Our galactic system consists, in fact, of two independent systems which are gradually travelling through each other, the faster system travelling directly away from Hercules with a velocity seventeen times greater than the slower system, which is making for a point near ι Ursæ Majoris.

Such an observation pleads eloquently for the view developed here—viz., that there are external galactic systems at a considerable distance from our own. For, if the systems had not been independent formerly, they could never have acquired the independent directions and velocities they actually exhibit.

We may take it, then, that our present visible universe is in process of transformation by the intrusion into it of an independent "galaxy" (as we may for short term a stellar system containing some 100 or 1000 million stars). There is, in fact, a "collision" of two galaxies—an event for which the chances at any time are less than 1 in 10 billion.

The existence of 100,000 million galaxies within

the supra-star to which we belong does not necessarily make any perceptible difference to our starry
heavens. Mr. R. A. Kennedy has shown[1] that an
infinite series of luminous universes of progressively
decreasing density would not perceptibly add to
the light we receive from the starry heavens.

It may here be objected that the vast times
required for the light of other bright galaxies to
reach us would in any case preclude our ever seeing
them. J. Ellard Gore, in his "Stellar Universe,"
p. 113, says: "We may further consider all the
systems of the second order as together forming a
system of the third order, and so on to the fourth
and higher orders. But we need not go further
than the third order, for if, as I have shown elsewhere, light would probably take millions of years
to reach us from an external universe of the second
order, surely the altogether inconceivable distance
of systems of the third order would sufficiently
account for their light not having yet reached us,
although travelling towards our earth for possibly
billions of years!"

I cannot accept the implied assumption that the
universe is finite in time. If light requires all that
time to reach us, what is there to prevent it? Time
is infinite, and its length is purely relative. We
shall, it is true, never see outlying galaxies as they
are, but as they were so many million or billion

---

[1] *English Mechanic*, No. 2194, April 22, 1907.

years ago. But so long as the probability of a
galaxy being bright is the same throughout space
and time, it does not matter at what particular
epoch any given galaxy shines out. The average
will hold good, and our argument will remain valid.

The Life of our Galaxy.—The question of a possible
"life" of the galactic system as an organism may at
first sight appear strange or even absurd; but can
we logically deny it, or even make it improbable?
The monist or materialist who analyses life into
matter and motion must find within our galaxy
sufficient of both to satisfy his most exacting conditions. Reduce sizes and times by the "world-
ratio," and what do we find? Some 1000 million
atoms in rapid motion, mostly forming binary
"molecules," but also clusters, chains, and solar
systems, with an inner "nucleus" and outer rim or
cell-wall sufficiently cohesive to exhibit individuality,
yet sufficiently open to admit material from outside
and even whole invading systems; a continuous
evolution of energy within, and a continuous exchange of energy with the outside world, showing
evidences just at present of a surplus of "imports"
over "exports."

Nothing is essentially altered by restoring this
"cell" to its original dimensions. What we lack at
present to complete the analogy is some evidence
of adaptation such as Herbert Spencer postulates
for all organic life. Such adaptation would, of

course, be so slow as to be practically unobservable. For one second of our time becomes 10^{22} seconds, or some 300 billion years in the time-scale of the higher world, and even the vast time required for the completion of the "invasion" now proceeding (say 20 billion years) is but a small fraction of a second in supra-time. In order to judge whether any of the motions actually observed among the stars can be equated with motions of atoms in a cell, we shall require some further information both concerning the actual configuration of atoms in a cell and concerning the conditions of life in the supra-world. Both these quests lie on the extreme borders of the territory surveyed by our present faculties; but that circumstance, while increasing the difficulty of such inquiry, also enhances its interest and importance.

Personally, I do not share the Haeckelian, monistic, or materialistic view. I prefer to look upon material phenomena as symbols of mental phenomena. Where there is motion there is thought. Where there is matter there is existence, conscious or sub-conscious. If at any time we succeed in accurately determining the configuration and motion of atoms in the human brain, we shall have an opportunity of interpreting the aspect of the heavens in terms of thought, of reading the thoughts of the world-soul, so to speak. But the human brain is, after all, only a very small portion of the thinking universe. Whole realms of potential or sub-conscious mental activity are stored away in more or less permanent configurations. Our conscious life is a very small part of our total life. We carry on vast activities which, having become automatic, no longer emerge above the level of consciousness. Our "life" comprehends the whole array of changes in the atomic structure of our physical organism, together with the sub-conscious mental activity represented by these changes, and the little gleam or "flicker" of conscious life at the top. If that is the case in ourselves, in what is to us the most familiar (or, indeed, the only familiar) part of the sentient universe, how can we expect to enter into the soul-life of the lower organisms, not to speak of so-called inorganic or "dead" matter? We should be chary of denying every species of life to an aggregation of matter simply because it is very bulky, and because its evolution is difficult to observe.

Supra-Light.—The supra-star is the largest body in the supra-world which we have as yet subjected to calculation. We have made its mass 10^{53} grammes and its diameter 10^{32} cm. But we can say a good deal more with a high degree of probability. Its temperature is enormous. By temperature we do not mean the kinetic energy of what we call atoms, but the kinetic energy of the "atoms" of the supra-world, these being what we call stars. The temperature of a body is the kinetic energy of its particles. Two particles may have very different masses but yet the same temperatures if their kinetic energies are the same —*i.e.*, if the product of the mass into the square of the velocity is the same for both particles. Now the average velocity of a hydrogen molecule at normal temperature and pressure is 169,400 cm. per second, and its mass is 1.1×10^{-24} gramme. The mass of the sun is 10^{34} grammes, or 10^{58} times that of a hydrogen molecule. Therefore its temperature as a "particle" would be the same if the square of its velocity were 10^{-58} times that of the hydrogen molecule, or if the velocity were 10^{-29} times that of the molecule. Instead of that, it is actually higher, being 1.99×10^6 cm. per second. Therefore we find that if stars are substituted for atoms in the supra-thermometer, the temperatures in the supra-world are altogether beyond what we observe in our world.

But the supra-stars are not necessarily luminous for all that. There is no necessary and unfailing connection between light and heat. Light consists of ether waves of a peculiar wave-length. Radiation in general consists of the vibrations of ether provoked by vibrations of electric charges. Without electrons or other elementary charges there can be neither light nor radiant heat. In the supra-world, the electrons are represented by planets. Now it

I

has been alleged that our solar system is rather an exception in our stellar universe, and that most stars are binaries, and probably unattended by planets. But the earth must be a radiator of supra-light. This is a matter admitting of no doubt whatever.

The earth carries round the sun annually a quantity of negative electricity, which makes its revolution equivalent to a current of 1 ampère. If the other planets also carry charges, the "supra-light" of the solar system will have a well-defined line spectrum. The wave-length of the supra-light emitted by the earth is 10^{18} cm.

On the whole the chances are just as much in favour of a starry vault in the supra-world as they are with us, since there is no essential change in the geometrical arrangement.

We cannot very well understand the conditions prevailing in our supra-star, except with reference to the sun. There also we have a gaseous body of very high temperature. If planets are rare accidents, then we may also look for planets in the supra-world; but a chance visit would not reveal them unless the circumstances were exceptionally favourable.

Our galactic system as a whole is most probably non-magnetic, though our solar system is undoubtedly a "molecular magnet." But the magnetic and other electric forces are very feeble on the astronomical scale, with the exception of radiation, which plays a part in astronomy of very sensible importance.

Both central and mechanical forces remain the same in the supra-world as in our galaxy. The dimensions are M^2L^{-2} and MLT^{-2} respectively, and since M, L, and T all change in the same ratio, the quantities are undisturbed.

So far, then, we can locate our supra-beings on supra-stars surrounded by a starry vault. What these supra-stars lack in density they more than compensate by their temperature—a process with which we are familiar in explosives.

CHAPTER V

LIFE IN THE SUPRA-WORLD

OUR speculations up to this have indicated, as the most probable structure of the universe beyond the stars, a collection of some 100,000 million galaxies, making up a "supra-star," and this supra-star forming the unit of a higher stellar universe, greatly resembling our own in outward appearance.

The ordinary common-sense difficulty which arises at once may be put in the form of the question: "Where are those 100,000 million galaxies? Why can we not see them?" The answer is, They are too far away. A simple calculation shows that our galaxy, when placed at the distance of the nearest outer galaxy (10^{28} cm.), would appear as a star of the 27th magnitude, and when placed at a distance equal to the radius of the supra-star it would appear as a star of the 51st magnitude—both magnitudes which are quite beyond our most powerful instruments. Indeed, all the stars and galaxies which constitute the supra-star, if lumped together and placed at the limit of our galaxy, would not be brighter than the moon; and if placed at the surface of the supra-star with ourselves in the centre, would dwindle to a body of the 21st magnitude, and the supra-star itself, seen from the next supra-star, would rank as a body of the 75th magnitude. That being the magnitude of the supra-star nearest our own, it is small wonder we do not see it. A supra-being would not, of course, see the supra-stars by our light, but by "supra-light," which may be powerful enough to reveal the existence of supra-stars to suitably-constructed sense organs.

Could we, by some superhuman power, condense our galactic system and seal it up in a tin can, we should, on looking round us, see nothing but utter darkness (barring the rare chance of some other galaxy being near). We should see nothing but a black void, though surrounded by 100,000 million shining galaxies constituting a supra-star, and by a trillion supra-stars constituting a body of the next higher order. The light to which, through countless ages, our eyes have learnt to respond, would utterly forsake us, and unless we were endowed with new retinas capable of responding to supra-light of wave-length 10^{18} cm., we should be practically blind. Such retinas would be impossible in our present bodies, with their rapid changes and short life-period. A single light-pulse would take a whole year to pass. We should, in fact, require supra-bodies, bodies in which the vital changes take place nearly a quadrillion times more slowly than they do in ours.

A body capable of life on the vast scale of a higher universe of this order must itself be commensurable with the supra-world. It must be a supra-organism.

Our galactic system is, in all probability, a supra-organism.—Let us picture to ourselves the conditions under which its life is carried on, in a world of a physical constitution such as our investigations have led us to assign to the supra-world.

Whatever is changed in passing from our world to the supra-world, the corresponding velocities remain the same. Atoms and stars, electrons and planets, cells and galaxies move with the same average absolute velocity in the same ether. This fact is mysterious, and, no doubt, significant. It provides us with a far-reaching uniformity of the first importance, a "pole at rest in the whirl of phenomena."

Distances being exaggerated 10^{22} times, it follows that times must be exaggerated in the same ratio, or the velocities would not be constant. But the measurement of space and time is purely relative. Time is measured by events, and any event which in our world requires one second, will, in the supra-world, require 10^{22} seconds for its accomplishment. But this vast period—over a hundred billion years—will, in the supra-world, only *appear* to be one second. It will contain the same number of corresponding events as does our second. Similarly,

10^{22} miles will contain the same number of corresponding objects as our single mile. We may, therefore, speak of a supra-second as an interval which plays the same part in the supra-world as one second does with us, so long as we remember that its actual length is 10^{22} of our seconds. Similarly, we may speak of supra-years, supra-miles, and supra-centimetres. Further, in order to make things more amenable to our imagination, we may mentally reduce the supra-world to our own dimensions simply by calling its supra-miles "miles." In this case we shall, so to speak, adopt the language of the supra-world itself. Then we should obtain the following description:—

"The galaxies have an average diameter of 1 millimetre, and are 10 kilometres (6·2 miles) apart. They move about with a speed of from 1 to 1000 metres per second. About every minute, or at least every hour, each galaxy approaches another galaxy, but rarely getting very near, and never colliding. Nearly a billion galaxies are confined within a sphere of the size of Saturn. This sphere may be called a 'supra-star.' The nearest similar sphere is one light-year away. The galaxies are loosely bound together by their gravitational attraction, which is compensated by a rotation of the supra-star accomplished in twenty-eight hours. Individual galaxies often fly out from the surface for some distance, but rarely far enough to be lost to

the supra-star. The galaxies darting about within
the sphere of the supra-star resemble a swarm
of gnats dancing in the sun."

Now, it has often been a subject of some curiosity
to know what these swarming gnats were doing.
Zoologists no doubt have their theories; but whatever they be, we can imagine that the gnats in their
sport are leading a very intense and presumably
joyous kind of life—a life in which considerations
of food play a very subordinate part.   Each gnat
consists of about a trillion atoms, arranged in cells
and groups fulfilling various functions, the chief
items of expenditure being connected with loco-
motive activities.   A small speck of protoplasm $0\cdot1$
micron in diameter contains as many atoms as
the Milky Way contains stars.   An amœba lives
in water, which shields it from the dire effects
of gravitational acceleration, and which, by its
dissociating power, furnishes it with certain ions
or chemical substances made appetising, so to speak,
by the relish of an electric charge.   Its own substance consists largely of water, which in its turn
consists of molecules, ternary stars, so to speak,
revolving almost in contact—two hydrogen satellites
about an oxygen sun.   When the amœba is hungry
it fuses its own body round about a desirable victim,
and absorbs a number of—star-clusters, shall we
say?—which, after a short sojourn among the
counter - attractions of the amœba's other star-

clusters, become less complex in structure, and are finally rejected, together with what remains of the victim after its useful clusters have been annexed.

Enlarge the amœba to the size of our galactic system, and you will have a starry vault more brilliant than ours, with stars more numerous and less far apart, but with the same stupendous majesty of motion and development, the same age-long evolution as ours. Its life will be as inscrutable, no more and no less, than the "life" of our own galaxy. We shall be just as unable to discern voluntary motion or trace the traffic of energy through the system. Possibly our galaxy has no voluntary motion. Its life may be more vegetative than animal. It may be concerned in building up elaborate structures rather than in undoing them. In any case, its life is bound to be what we call intense or strenuous. Life is measured intensively by the number and variety of experiences crowded into a given time. This number and variety, as our calculations have tended to show, is very great in the supra-world. A roving galaxy has, so to speak, a lively time of it. Taking the word "life" in its very widest sense, as a registering and utilisation of experiences, and including among the latter conscious, sub-conscious, and "material" effects, there is every justification for applying the term "life" to the existence and development of our own or any other galaxy. The only reasonable doubt applies to the degree of consciousness with which that life is endowed.

It is not for us, who spend a third of our lives in a state of unconscious, or at most, subconscious, activity, to determine the limit of consciousness in other beings. We do not know, and cannot say, from our standpoint outside, how far the life of an amœba or a protococcus may be governed by judgment and choice, or how far it may differ from ours in our rare moments of full self-consciousness. The area and scope of our own consciousness is constantly shifting. Our consciousness is merged in a sea of conscious existence, just as our body is immersed in a material universe. Every man with a philosophic, as distinguished from a mechanically scientific, training knows that the two parallel universes—those of consciousness and of matter—are coextensive and interpenetrating; are, in fact, two aspects of the same reality. No portion of matter is entirely independent of other matter. No so-called "individual" consciousness is entirely independent of other mental existences. In ourselves, but in nothing else, we are in touch with both aspects, both universes. When we perceive other material existences, we ascribe consciousness to them to the extent to which their material structure and activity resembles ours, but no further. That is our prejudice. It is a very natural prejudice, and only becomes mischievous when elevated into a dogma, and used in order to deny consciousness where we have no real evidence against it.

If our galaxy is not conscious yet, it may be in the process of acquiring consciousness. The curious evolution discovered by Kapteyn and Eddington is very suggestive of some crisis. The mingling of two galactic systems may be the equivalent of the process by which the amœba acquires star-clusters of superior vital value. Or it may be an act of a great Birth—a mingling of two germ-cells to form a more self-determining being. The interpenetration may be estimated to occupy a thousand million years—a very small fraction of a supra-second. In that time the two galaxies will have brought their accumulated individual experience to bear upon each other, and will be prepared to face life with a superior endowment and a better prospect of self-determination. Such a prospect is surely quite as conceivable as the simplest process of generation such as we can see accomplish itself under the microscope in a few minutes.

But what about ourselves in this gigantic birth? What part have we to play in the next thousand million years? Will *our* accumulated experience be a part of the dowry of that great being which is now being born in the heavens?

This brings me to what will most likely be considered the wildest and most fanciful part of the speculations suggested by the present line of reason-

ing. Where nothing is certain we may as well
discard all prudent reservations. It will save time
if I state a vague possibility in language of positive conviction. All the usual reservations may
therefore, in what follows in the next chapter, be
"taken as read."

CHAPTER VI

THE CONQUEST OF THE SUPRA-WORLD

THE human race has evolved on a small planet in the solar system in the course of several million years of organic life. Its destiny is to combine with other sentient beings to govern the solar system, the solar cluster, and finally the new galaxy now being evolved.

In the course of his triumphant career, man has succeeded in extending his personality far beyond the limits of his body. If by " personality " in the wider sense we understand all material things controlled by the individual, then we must include his clothes, his property, and his whole sphere of influence under that term. Individuals vary enormously in the extent of this wider " personality," much more widely than they do in their physical organisation. But every community has its " personality " also.

It controls the " personalities " of its individuals to the same extent as it controls their minds—at least on the average, and in the long run. The community is an individual of a higher order, with a consciousness distributed over the aggregate consciousness, and a "personality" of power and possession gathered from the aggregate of its members.

A nation is an individual of a still higher order, controlling not only the mental and physical life of a vast number of human beings, but a correspondingly large portion of land. Nations, like crowds, have their psychology. They are born, and live, and die. They have passions and greeds and diseases, and sometimes generous impulses. The human personality is coextensive with the visible universe in one sense already. It is destined to become so in a much more practical sense. Man governs the earth. It is changing its face for him. Other beings are flourishing or disappearing at his pleasure. Soon he will govern the more powerful elements, the sea and the wind, and the heat of the sun.

By-and-by, also, the earth will show signs of becoming uninhabitable. He will readjust it, and bring it nearer to the sun or further away. More likely, perhaps, he will discover that Jupiter offers superior inducements to colonists, or he will come to some understanding with the inhabitants of Jupiter, if such there be, with regard to future co-operation. It is pretty certain that nothing will bar the conquering march of human intelligence, except a similar intelligence. Either man will come upon a civilisation resembling his own or he will not. In the former case he will, after a trial of strength, perhaps, ally himself with that other race. In the latter alternative he will mould all matter to his will. He will control the sun with a switch like an electric lamp. His physical acts will require a minimum expenditure of energy; but they will let loose or guide all the huge forces of the universe. In proceeding to greater conquests, man simply draws upon the almighty power within him. He is not alone in either world, material or mental. He has infinite reserves in both. His physical organism is specially adapted to the conquest of the earth. When he proceeds to greater spheres it may change; but the change, we may anticipate, will not be as great as his change of power. Man's powers have been extended within the last centuries in enormous disproportion to any changes in his body. In proceeding to control the solar system, man may develop, or rather resume, powers now found only in a rudimentary form. In taking control of nature, man has lost many spiritual gifts once possessed by his ancestors. Clairvoyance and telepathy were once almost universal. They have been deliberately atrophied in order to fit man for the conquest of nature. The human mind not only requires delicate senses and perceptions; it also requires certain blindnesses and insensibilities. Some sensibilities have been crusted over. Man has become a crustacean as regards some of his faculties. These have become "occult." When they are once more required they will again come forth. They are beginning to come forth now.

When activities have to be spread over geological periods instead of lifetimes, man will, in order to cope with them, either have to prolong his life, or find a new way of permanently recording his experiences. Both ends may possibly be accomplished by a thinning of the veil which divides embodied man from the accumulated intelligence of his ancestors, who poured forth by the million every year into that unknown realm of existence with which the human race, for good reasons of its own, has severed almost all conscious connection.

The result will be, in any case, that the solar system will become *conscious*. It will control its own destiny, and choose among the energies in the universe those best adapted to preserve its continuity of evolution.

Can anything more be accomplished in the time at our disposal, in a thousand million years? It would not be too much to assume that the scale of operations will extend as the basis expands. When the planets move "like one man," when the solar system is instinct with life, it will develop new powers. Born into the solar cluster, it will endeavour to adapt itself to its surroundings, and then

to adapt its surroundings to itself.   An outside
spectator might look as fruitlessly for the seat of
the solar "soul" as he does for the human soul in
the cells of the brain.   He would note certain activities and adaptations, and if they resembled his
own he would postulate life or even consciousness.
He might notice a growth of the single system into
a cluster of systems, or the break-up of several
systems to form another system on a higher scale.
Our imagination almost forsakes us at this point,
until we arrive at the borders of the galaxy, and
behold ! we have again a living thing, like the
amœba under the cover-glass, which is as wonderful as a living galaxy, and fraught with infinitely
greater possibilities than a dead galaxy.   But in
this vast process just sketched, which has taken a
thousand million years to accomplish itself, *a living
being has been born into the supra-world*, there to
live a life akin to that of our earthly organisms,
but extending over practically infinite time, and
counting its seconds by the parade of galaxies.   Its
long evolution, the " Conquest of the Supra-world,"
will count as an insignificant fraction of a second—
a mere nothing.   It will, in its own estimation, have
been born afresh at a definite and sharply defined
epoch, with no assignable pre-existence.   It will
enter upon its vivid life in the supra-world, conscious of the all-absorbing Present, and oblivious
of the ages during which it was slowly and labori-

K

ously evolved into a higher life out of the strenuous life of the human race.

And the supra-man, studying the little captured galaxy in his microscope, will wonder if the little thing has any intelligence or consciousness, or if it is only "matter and motion," with hard round atoms knocking up against each other and occasionally phosphorescing into "thought."

CHAPTER VII

THE CHAIN OF UNIVERSES

A GENERAL survey of the ground covered by these investigations shows that they necessitate a revision of hitherto-accepted views in those departments of science and philosophy which deal with the infinite and the infinitesimal, and, generally speaking, with space and time in the abstract. The relativity of space and time itself, always accepted as an axiom, is here for the first time carried to its logical conclusion, and given a physical interpretation. It would have been easy, and also somewhat fashionable, to extend the limits of space by breaking down its three-dimensional character. Greater freedom of hypothesis, and greater security from criticism, might also have been obtained by abrogating other fundamental laws of nature. But the experience of mankind is opposed to any such proceeding. When Newton first extended the earth's attraction as far as the moon his hypothesis appeared far-fetched and presumptuous. But we have gone much further since, and have learned more and more that the strange and the wonderful must not be looked for beyond the stars. The abysses of space are no more strange and formidable than a river-bed or a snow-drift. There is no problem on an infinite scale which is not equally presented to us on an infinitesimal scale. If we can unravel the secrets of matter down to the molecule and up to the star-cluster, we shall know the secrets of all matter to the uttermost ends of space and time. Our faculties will have grasped the material universe. This prospect is magnificent and encouraging. It holds out a vast promise, and indicates a speedy fulfilment of it. The results achieved will be utterly independent of space and time. The laws of the material universe as disclosed to us by our faculties will rule for ever. Could we by any chance catch a glimpse of our starry heavens as they will appear in a trillion years, or as they appeared a trillion years ago, we might fail to recognise its constellations; but the stars would be shining as they shine upon us now, with their different spectra and magnitudes, their orbits, and their proper motions. The laws of chemistry and of physics would still hold good, and those of geology and biology would be the same wherever the local circumstances were similar to those of our earth. This eternity of the material universe gives a new dignity to it and to our work in solving its riddles. We find that the structure of the material universe is consistent with its general stability. True, we cannot yet trace the circulation of energy in all its course. We do not yet know how the radiation of light and heat is kept up indefinitely. But if energy is indestructible, as we believe it is, it is clear that even in an infinite universe there must be some circulation of it. The energy whose dissipation we observe is, after all, the energy, not of our world, but of the infra-world, which alone provides us with light and radiant heat ; and that same world, as we know from the phenomena of radio-activity, has reserves of energy which are but rarely tapped, and which may possibly in future be traced to the radiant energy dissipated into space.

The realisation of the infra-world and the supra-world amounts to a vast extension of the scope of the laws of nature. But, on the other hand, it opposes a decided barrier to their indefinite simplification. It has been a favourite idea with biologists that all vital phenomena can ultimately be reduced to the configuration and motion of atoms. With an almost pathetic faith, grotesquely out of keeping with their boasted scepticism, they have for several generations past been clinging to this dogma. The chemist, that most practical of men of science, has preferred to deal with phenomena as they appeared to his senses and became amenable to his balance, burette, and thermometer. The physicist, working on the very borderland of science, always in touch with ultimate foundations, and surrounded by the incomprehensible, has almost developed into a mystic. He has shattered the atom, and is now endeavouring to reduce matter to some unintelligible turbulence in an inconceivable ether. He is on a fool's errand. "That way madness lies." It is sheer waste of time to look for an ultimate particle, or for a continuous fluid of certain density or elasticity. We can never arrive at anything ultimate by making our unit small. There will always be something a million times smaller, infinitely smaller. Why not, then, take the bull by the horns and recognise that dimensions are only relative, that our faculties have a limited range, and that, however far we extend that range on a larger or smaller scale, the same problems are presented to us? Let us not bury these problems out of sight in the Infinitesimal. No material interpretation of the universe will ever explain anything. The elementary particle, the elementary position or motion, will be the greatest of all puzzles. Real progress must be sought for in quite another direction.

Let us by all means reduce the number of laws to the minimum. Let us, if we can, explain gravitation by ether motion; but if we fail, if we have to admit universal gravitation as an ultimate and irreducible reality, where is the loss? We must have some fundamental assumptions, incapable of further explanation, and none are likely to be much simpler than Newton's law. The ether might also be taken for granted, and without any further speculations as to its constitution, we may assume that the velocity of light is a definite and most important constant, more important than ever since our discovery that it is both relatively and absolutely the same in the three worlds.

A few such fundamental principles may enable us by-and-by to marshal all phenomena in due order, and to survey them in proper perspective. But when it comes to the explanation, or, rather, the interpretation, of these fundamental principles, material conceptions are no longer useful. The fundamental principles are necessarily functions of the five senses with which we happen to be endowed. They are the symbols which connect our physical organism with the realities outside us. Any further reduction must be accompanied by an analysis of our own senses and faculties. Not microscopy, but psychology, will solve the "Riddle of the Universe."

Even in dealing with ordinary sensation we are constantly coming upon sources of error, such as malobservation, illusion, and hallucination. The senses require constant correction and supervision by the intellect. Not by a single intellect either, for no fact, observed and recorded by even the most famous and best trained observer, is ever accepted on his unsupported testimony alone, but by the combined intellect of those supposed to be best qualified to judge. Witness Blondlot's "N-rays" and Secchi's Martian canals.

In searching for ultimate truth, we have to bring our higher intellectual faculties into play. We have to investigate those "laws of cognition" which govern the acquisition of knowledge in general. We have to concentrate ourselves in our own higher selves, and watch our ordinary faculties at work, just as those faculties watch our sensations, and our senses in their turn watch the world. And in doing so, we are gradually and inevitably drawn to the conclusion that mind is everything, and matter but an expression of the universal mind. A table, a house, a machine is the embodiment of some human mind. A stone is the embodiment of some mind at present inaccessible to us, of some will at present inscrutable. Matter signifies existence—life independent of ourselves, but subject to our will under certain conditions, just as men are to some extent. Motion means change or experience. Inertia means habit. The ether means, perhaps, the all-embracing, all-connecting over-soul of the universe. Radiation means, perchance, the intercommunication of smaller minds.

Here we enter upon that virgin field where, I believe, the science of the future will blossom forth. In entering upon it, a new perspective opens out, a perspective infinitely more glorious than the starry host visible to our human eyes. We breathe a higher and purer air—an air of freedom, of infinite life and power and greatness, unfettered by the shackles of our earthly existence. Many of the sons of men, in all ages, have caught glimpses of such a higher existence. It is open to all of us and, I believe, destined for all. But its possibility and prospect need not draw us away from the present phase prematurely. Like devotees of chess or football, we descend into the arena and consent to be bound for a time by more or less absurd restrictions. We "play the game." And that game has always been played, and will always be played. It is a necessary discipline and liberal education.

We are for a time placed at some point in the chain of material universes, an infinite series of which, strange to say, can, as we have seen, occupy the same space at the same time. We are planted on the crust of a planet. It is a curious form of existence; but we know of no other. Our faculties can dimly perceive a corresponding existence on the next lower order of planetary or stellar units, on electrons or atoms. But no corresponding possibility is reached on a larger scale until we reach the supra-star, the stellar unit of the supra-world. Our faculties can, with the utmost effort, just perceive three links of the chain, and only one with fair completeness. But that is enough. It gives a complete "cross-section" of the material universe. Having exhausted the lessons of this cross-section, we can proceed to other types of universes, at present (to us) non-material, and more or less immaterial.

Of one thing, however, we may be certain: No universe exists which is entirely unconnected with this of ours. We know that the fruit of our slightest act goes thundering down the ages, that nothing is ever effaced, that everything is of infinite and eternal consequence. And if it leaves a permanent mark on the material universe, it will affect, also, all invisible universes. This reflection may give a new zest to our present form of existence. To pierce into the innermost recesses of nature, to mould natural forces to our will, to make life happy and glorious for ourselves and our kind, to assert our supremacy over disease and death, to conquer and rule the universe in virtue of the infinite power within us—such is our task here and now.

It is being more and more consciously taken in hand by the human race—a race which, since its earliest origins, has numbered about a billion individuals. The aggregate lives of these individuals cover a vast variety of experiences and circumstances, and the record of those experiences is embodied in our own physical organisms and other records more or less permanent. The human race has hurled itself against the fastnesses of nature and captured them one by one. The war has been a record of blood and tears. But in the new generation the wounds are healed and the tears are dried, and the battle is renewed. Man emerges from each successive conflict stronger, saner, and better, more assured of ultimate victory, fitter to reap the fruits of it. The individual suffers, and dies a million deaths, but his misery is but a drop in the ocean of his happiness. His pain is never infinite. Like all bodily sensations, it has its maximum, beyond which no power can intensify it. Death itself is peaceful, painless, free from all fear. The fear passes away when it is no longer useful as a stimulus to activity. The barriers of the human world fall away. The "game" is played to the last. Once more the individual is withdrawn towards that centre of sentient life where all souls are one with the great Over-soul. What his future fate may be we need not now inquire. Should it ever become necessary to enter upon and pursue such inquiry, we may be sure that a full acquaintance with the laws of our present visible universe will form the best preparation for it. And these laws we shall apply with the greater confidence when we know that they suffice to interpret not only our own universe, but the two other worlds just discernible on the horizon of our present faculties.

APPENDIX

SYSTEM OF MEASUREMENT AND NOTATION

As is usual in scientific works, the metric system has been adopted here. The measures of length and weight may be assumed to be familiar. The "dyne" is the unit of force, and is the 981st part of a gramme. The "erg" is the unit of work, and is the work involved in proceeding against a force of 1 dyne through the distance of 1 cm. Thus, 981 ergs are expended in lifting 1 gramme through 1 centimetre.

The exponential notation is the only system suitable for the work in this book. The index or "exponent" indicates how many times we must multiply the number by itself. When the number is 10, it indicates the number of ciphers in the result. Thus $10^2 = 100$; $10^6 = 1,000,000$. Two such "powers" of 10 are multiplied by simply adding their indices; $10^2 \times 10^6 = 10^8$.

The negative index implies a reciprocal value. Thus $10^{-2} = \frac{1}{10^2}$ or 0·01. In this case, the index gives the number of ciphers preceding the digit in the decimal fraction.

The space saved by exponential notation may be realised by remembering that 10^{53} would be a number of 54 figures in ordinary notation, and would not fit in this line.

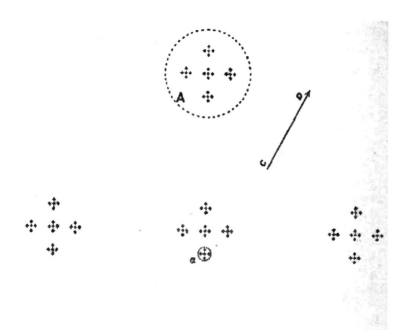

DIAGRAM OF A MULTI-UNIVERSE

IN the accompanying diagram a multi-universe is shown, constructed upon a cruciform or octahedral principle. Though this is not the plan of the infra-world or the supra-world, the diagram is useful in showing that an infinite series of similar successive universes may exist without producing a "blazing sky." If the smallest visible crosses represent atoms of the infra-world, the figure enclosed by the circle a represents a star of the infra-world or an atom of our world. A would then correspond to a star of our world, and the whole diagram would represent a "supra-star." The "world-ratio" in this case is 7, instead of 10^{22}, as in reality. Successive world-spheres, like a, A, &c., enclose 7 times as much matter as the sphere next below. *The matter in each world-sphere is proportional to its radius*, and its density is inversely proportional to its surface. This is the condition required for fulfilling the laws of gravitation and radiation. In the direction CD the sky will appear quite black, although there is an infinite succession of universes.

Printed by BALLANTYNE, HANSON & Co.
Edinburgh & London

CPSIA information can be obtained
at www.ICGtesting.com
Printed in the USA
BVHW041050100920
588542BV00004B/101

9 781375 942584